BREAKING & ENTERING

UNLOCKING YOUR PATH TO POWER THROUGH MENTORSHIP

Dr. Misty R. Sharp Ladd, CPP, PCI, PSP

BREAKING & ENTERING:
UNLOCKING YOUR PATH TO POWER THROUGH MENTORSHIP

DR. MISTY R. SHARP LADD, CPP, PCI, PSP

Cover Design & Formatting by 100Covers
Professional Editing by Catt Editing
Back Cover Photo by Nelly Hernandez Photography

For more information: Misty@BreakingAndEnteringBook.com

eBook ISBN: 979-8-9902180-0-0
Paperback ISBN: 979-8-9902180-1-7

Ready to take the challenge?

Unlock your power: Find your mentor in 30 days or less using these easy-to-follow action cards!

Maximize your mentoring relationship with just 5–15 minutes a day. Dive into tasks that cover mindset, momentum, and mentorship! Stay on track with these actionable steps for consistent growth with these Mentee Minutes action cards (Mentor Minute Power Packs also available) designed to provide you with bite-sized tasks that can make a powerful impact on career growth!

To Get Your Free Resources:

SCAN ME!

DEDICATION

To my dearest daughter, Megan: You are the radiant star that has illuminated my path and filled my life with boundless joy. Your unwavering support, resilience, and the unwritten chapters of your future inspire me to reach higher and dream bigger. Words can never truly capture the depth of pride I feel in you. You are not only my proudest accomplishment but the very essence of my life's most profound fulfillment.

To my loving parents, Gil and Olivia: Your guidance, wisdom, and endless love have been the foundation upon which my journey to success has been built. Your sacrifices and unending encouragement are cherished beyond words.

To my cherished sister, Wendy, and her beautiful family: Alex, Cole, and Lily. Your warmth, camaraderie, and the love that binds us together have made my life all the more meaningful. The laughter and epic time we share together fills my heart with joy. Your presence in my life is a constant reminder of the importance of family and shared dreams.

To my large, lovable group of family and friends: Your unwavering support and the Bond we share are a source of strength and inspiration. The echoes of your encouragement and the shared stories of our paths have provided the backdrop for my aspirations. I am profoundly grateful for the love, unity, and praise that you have poured into my life.

To the source of all blessings, God's favor: With gratitude in my heart, I acknowledge the divine favor that has guided me through every twist and turn of life's intricate narrative. Your grace is the unspoken force behind my endeavors.

May the words in these pages stand as a testament to the collective love, support, and divine guidance that continue to shape my journey. It is with boundless love and appreciation that I dedicate this book to you all.

CONTENTS

Dedication v

Acknowledgments ix

Preface xi

Unlocking the Power Within 1

Chapter 1: The Power of the Ask 7

Chapter 2: The Power of Yes 17

Chapter 3: The Power of Books 23

Chapter 4: The Power of Certification 31

Chapter 5: The Power of the Underdog 41

Chapter 6: The Power of Organizations & Service 49

Chapter 7: The Power of Action & Delegation 61

Chapter 8: The Power of Diversity 67

Chapter 9: The Power of No 73

Embracing the Power & Beyond 81

Connect with Me! 87

Author Biography 89

ACKNOWLEDGMENTS

It's important to recognize that my journey has been influenced by countless individuals, many of whom won't be named in these pages. This omission is not meant to diminish their profound impact on my life and career.

I want to extend my heartfelt gratitude to my fellow members of the book club at Big Idea to Bestseller, a community led by the inspiring Jake Kelfer and his dedicated team. Their unwavering support and guidance were instrumental at every step of this book's journey. This project, a dream I've held close for decades, would not have seen the light of day without their encouragement and collective wisdom. Let's go!

In the company of exceptional authors within this exclusive club, I found not only motivation but a shared dedication to making a positive impact on people's lives. It's this shared mission that fueled my commitment to completing this book swiftly, with the hope that it could begin enriching and transforming the lives of its readers right now. To my weekly accountability writing partner, Jai Michaels, you have been a rock of consistency, I cannot wait to witness the compassionate leadership that your book will undoubtedly inspire. To Telma Sanchez and Dr. Jen Mott, I would like to extend my heartfelt appreciation for your invaluable support and inspiration throughout the writing process.

The post-writing process has been smooth and fantastic thanks to several professionals that I want to mention. First, Carly Catt, you have been a dream to work with, your poise and professionalism have been impeccable from the moment I reached out to you. Your deliberate and polished systematic approach instilled confidence in the outcome of this part of this crazy journey. Your kind and thoughtful editing has undoubtedly made me look wiser and more capable than I am. I cannot wait to work with you again soon (if you need an editor, you should work with her too, www.cattediting.com)!

Shadda Siega-Alinson, my project manager at 100Covers, when I thought I had blown my timeline you and your team made sure that we pulled it off. Words cannot explain how excited I was to work with Nelly Hernandez. After being a raging fan of @NellyHernandezPhotography for many years, to get my turn in front of your lens was beyond fabulous! Finally, Chris N. Cheetham-West, MBA—for you to take the time to review my book when you are busy releasing your own audiobook between globe-trotting keynote speaking engagements was incredibly generous of you. You have been *Leading in a Virtual World* and I've been learning (@ChrisNWest)!

Most importantly, I want to acknowledge you, the reader. Your decision to invest time and effort in self-improvement is a powerful testament to your passion and unwavering drive for success. Whether you are a business leader, an entrepreneur, a student, a mentor, or a mentee, your commitment to reaching the next level is admirable. I commend you for your dedication to personal and professional growth, and I'm honored that you've chosen to take this journey with me.

PREFACE

I want to emphasize that the knowledge and insights I'm about to share with you have been forged over more than three decades, marked by blood, sweat, tears, a fair amount of colorful language, and more than my fair share of failures. Perhaps one of my best (and occasionally worst) traits is an unyielding persistence (on my good days, I think resilience). Many of the innovative concepts and strategies I will present have taken me a considerable amount of time to discover and implement. The great news, however, is that you do not have to follow my same winding path.

I once had a quote pinned to my very first office desk after college, and it read, "It's not about the destination, it's about the journey." To this day, I firmly believe in this philosophy. Each one of us is on a unique journey, and that's something to celebrate. However, I want to encourage you to use this book as a shortcut—a way to bypass some of those challenging years, to leap right into the exciting and epic chapters of your own story.

By immersing yourself in the pages that follow, you can harness the power of the nine actionable lessons that have guided my path to success.

As you delve into this book, my hope is that you'll find not only inspiration but also practical wisdom that propels you forward, allowing you to navigate your unique journey with greater speed and fewer encounters with metaphorical "swamps" teeming with "gators and mosquitos." Together, let's journey toward your fullest potential and the epic adventures that lie ahead.

You can read this book in any order. I have written it in chronological order; however, one chapter title may speak to you first. This is your resource; I want to encourage you to use it to help you in your unique journey. Take notes, share the contents, and utilize the action steps and resources to your full benefit. The structural layout of the book is as follows:

- Chapter title
- Mentor story
- Resources for action steps
- Quote
- Psychology key (a source for additional research if interested)

Unlocking the Power Within

Misty Sharp, The Unlikely Doctor

What You Stand to Gain by Following the Guidance in This Book . . . Welcome to a journey unlike any other. As you embark on these pages, you are not just opening a book; you're breaking and entering into a world where the rules of achievement are rewritten, where success is not confined to the narrow corridors of convention. You are stepping into a realm where the power to transform your life resides within you, waiting to be unleashed.

Hello, I'm Misty, I sit before you as a testament to the extraordinary potential that lies within every one of us. I started my professional journey as a private investigator and faced obstacles that would have made many falter. But through the power of mentorship and unwavering determination, I broke through barriers, shattered expectations, and achieved what some might consider impossible.

In the tapestry of my life, threads of adversity, determination, and unwavering ambition have woven a story of resilience and achievement. As a pregnant teenager at seventeen facing a future veiled in uncertainty, I embarked on a journey that would redefine the limits of possibility. Navigating the stormy weather of an abusive marriage, I found strength I never knew I possessed. With each challenge I encountered, I grew more determined to reclaim control of my destiny. As a first-generation college student, I ventured into uncharted territory, driven by a relentless desire to create a better life not just for myself but for my daughter.

Amid the shadows of uncertainty, mentors emerged as guiding lights, illuminating the path before me. Their wisdom and encouragement nurtured the flicker of hope within, igniting a fire that would propel me forward. Their belief in my potential (even when I could not see it myself) transformed my doubts into determination and my fears into fuel for growth.

My early days as a security guard earning minimum wage could have been career quicksand. However, these mentors painted a canvas of possibility before me. Their guidance instilled the conviction that no dream was too audacious to pursue. In a career field dominated by men, I carved my own path, climbing the ladder of success. One pinnacle of this journey was earning the elite status that only a few women in the world have ever achieved, the ASIS Triple Crown certification, a milestone that would not have been possible without the mentors who championed me.

I embarked on the challenging road to a PhD in the pursuit of knowledge. Embracing education as a means to shatter stereotypes, I stepped confidently into the world of criminal justice and forensic psychology. As I faced academic rigor and juggled responsibilities, the seeds of transformation were sown, culminating in my attainment of a doctorate. My family and mentors were the pillars of power upon which I leaned.

Yet, my intention is not to boast. Rather, it is to illuminate the extraordinary potential that lies within each of us, waiting to be awakened by the guidance of those who have walked the path before us. The mentors who shaped my journey were pivotal in my transformation. Their belief in my abilities and their willingness to share their wisdom propelled me beyond boundaries. The path I tread is a reminder that success can be born from adversity and that dreams can flourish amid challenges. I share my journey not as a rare exception but as a testament to the power of the human spirit inside each of us.

Your journey, no matter its beginnings or where it is now, holds the promise of remarkable growth and triumph. Let these stories be a beacon that guides you through your own extraordinary adventure, guided by the wisdom and support of mentors who believe in your potential. My hope is that my story serves as a source of inspiration for those who dare to chase their dreams against all odds. Together, we can rewrite the narratives of our lives, transforming challenges into powerful progress toward achievement.

This book is about more than the mentor–mentee relationship. Reading this journey, and taking the recommended actions, could inspire countless individuals in myriad careers to learn to invest in themselves in three areas that truly matter most: health, wealth, and relationships. If I could pinpoint one perfect candidate to benefit from unlocking the powerful keys to follow, it would be the solopreneur who wants to scale their business to make more time for their family, to create more opportunities in their community, and to establish their financial independence. This book speaks to the power needed to create the most advantageous mindset, develop a unique roadmap specifically for your journey, and perform the action steps to take to align with the best mentor for you.

In this book, I'll share how I harnessed these nine powers that defined my path to success. These powers are not mystical, nor are they reserved for a select few. They are principles, strategies, and insights that anyone can embrace to propel themselves toward triumph.

The Power of the Ask: Discover how the simple act of asking can open doors you never thought possible.

The Power of Yes: Learn how saying yes to opportunities, even when they seem daunting, can lead to remarkable growth.

The Power of Books: Explore the transformative potential of knowledge and how books can fuel your mentor relationships.

The Power of Certification: Uncover the significance of expertise and how certifications can elevate your career.

The Power of the Underdog: Embrace the underdog within and turn adversity into your greatest strength.

The Power of Organizations & Service: Understand the role of organizations and service in building a legacy of success.

The Power of Action & Delegation: Master the art of taking action and delegating effectively to achieve your goals.

The Power of Diversity: Embrace diversity as a source of strength and innovation.

The Power of No: Learn when and how to say no to focus on what truly matters.

Through each chapter, you will gain practical insights, strategies, and real-world examples to fuel your own unconventional journey. This is not a book about conforming; it's a guide to tapping into your unique strengths and forging your path to success, whatever that may look like for you. As you read, you will discover that success is not defined by someone else's standards or the number of followers on social media. It is about harnessing your inner power, creating your definition of achievement, and pursuing it with unwavering determination. I am confident that when you apply these power principles to the areas of your life that matter most to you, the progress will be profound! A sample of the readers I had specifically in mind while authoring this book were those who are . . .

- **Feeling Stuck in Conventional Paths:** those frustrated with following traditional paths that haven't led to the success they desire, seeking a way out of their comfort zones
- **Lack of Mentorship:** those struggling to find mentors who truly understand their aspirations and can provide an effective partnership through guidance
- **Fear of Failure:** those held back by fear of failure or the unknown and need strategies to overcome these fears and take calculated risks
- **Difficulty Balancing Life and Success:** those who may be conflicted about achieving success without compromising their personal values, someone who is looking for ways to achieve more without losing themselves in the process

Many people equate success solely with fame, wealth, and widespread recognition, often influenced by the curated images on social media. True success and achievement encompass a much broader spectrum. They involve personal growth, overcoming challenges, fulfilling meaningful goals, giving back to your community, and finding happiness and contentment on one's unique journey. While financial success can be part of the picture, it does not define the entirety of achievement. Each person's path is distinct, and success should align with one's values and aspirations, not conform to external standards. By showcasing many of my personal experiences with my mentors, I will illustrate how the mentor–mentee relationship has not only impacted my career but has led to fulfillment and meaningful accomplishments outside the mainstream definitions of success.

Are you ready to break and enter into a world of limitless possibilities? Ready to overcome adversity and make a positive impact? Are you prepared to rewrite the rules and embark on your extraordinary journey? If you're looking for a one-and-done secret formula to make a million dollars in a month, you might want to check your fairy godmother's reading list. Here is the exciting news: this book is about real progress, not just magical shortcuts. This book can be your roadmap, not the final destination. If you're ready to roll up your sleeves, implement some action steps, and find an incredible mentor who is as invested in your journey as you are, you will be a whole lot closer to success than where you started. If so, let's begin. Your powerful transformation starts now.

"The people closest to me determine my level of success or failure. The better they are, the better I am. And if I want to go to the highest level, I can do it only with the help of other people. We have to take each other higher." **—John C. Maxwell**

Get Your *Free* Mentor–Mentee Deliverables Checklist Here

To Get Your Free Resources:

SCAN ME!

CHAPTER 1

The Power of the Ask

Steve Coppinger, The State Trooper

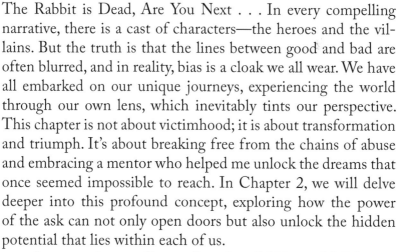

The Rabbit is Dead, Are You Next . . . In every compelling narrative, there is a cast of characters—the heroes and the villains. But the truth is that the lines between good and bad are often blurred, and in reality, bias is a cloak we all wear. We have all embarked on our unique journeys, experiencing the world through our own lens, which inevitably tints our perspective. This chapter is not about victimhood; it is about transformation and triumph. It's about breaking free from the chains of abuse and embracing a mentor who helped me unlock the dreams that once seemed impossible to reach. In Chapter 2, we will delve deeper into this profound concept, exploring how the power of the ask can not only open doors but also unlock the hidden potential that lies within each of us.

I grew up in a small town (less than 5,000 people). My parents were loving and hardworking family folks who managed to raise two incredibly determined young women. Determination and persistence are most frequently listed in the "win" column of personality traits; however, when left frustrated by many of the limitations of a small, rural community, these traits gave me an unbridled desire to break free. Free from the confines of my upbringing. I wanted to do or be anything other than the ordinary. I was not a reader; I had no patience for it. I wanted to seek experiences. I liked dangerous people and situations. I will skip those details as my parents might read this book.

It is safe to say that these desires led me down an unexpected path. At a tender age, I fell in love with an older local, a choice that led me into marriage at just seventeen. Months away from my eighteenth birthday, I made the decision not to drop out of school and pursue a GED.

There were no other students in my gifted and talented courses who had ever dared to walk the halls pregnant. It was such a rare event that when I went to school to receive my schedule and locker for the year, I had a bottom locker, which the school said I could not exchange for a top locker because those were "the rules." Luckily, a delightful transfer student from a larger city had started and had the locker above me; without even a second's hesitation, he moved my books to his locker so I wouldn't have to bend over to retrieve my books from the floor.

My honeymoon unveiled a harsh truth—my husband was a relentless alcoholic (and a mean drunk). Struggling with the weight of this revelation, I chose not to disclose it to my family. In my naivety, I believed he would change, and I didn't want my family to harbor ill feelings toward their granddaughter's father. I missed only two weeks of school with the birth of my daughter. This quick return was possible due to my youth and my mother's willingness to keep Megan while I was in class.

Balancing college and having a child was no small feat. I had never babysat growing up, nor had I had a job. Now, virtually overnight, I was forced to learn how to be a mom, wife, college student, and employee. I didn't even know how to boil an egg (and we didn't have the internet!). These many areas of uncharted waters collide with the ever-growing threats of abuse.

At just nine months old, my daughter took her first steps while I struggled to grow up myself. To make ends meet, I had to work a full-time job and relied on daycare, as leaving my baby with an unemployed alcoholic was simply not an option.

As I exponentially learned more about life, my husband's jealousy of my work and education grew, leading to escalating verbal threats and frequent emotional abuse. These acts of intimidation often occurred just before important tests or as I strived to complete demanding projects.

My initial goal of becoming a pharmacist became increasingly difficult to chase, and I ultimately lost my scholarship due to the overwhelming workload. With determination, I shifted my focus to a degree in accounting, where my proficiency in math offered a glimmer of hope. However, I quickly learned that accounting is about far more than numbers. I think you will understand why it was not a good fit for me when I tell you I still do not balance my checkbook, nor can I do my own taxes. Still, in the midst of this dark academic journey, I found an unexpected ray of sunshine.

In my accounting courses, I crossed paths with a remarkable friend, Peppi Coppinger. Our shared experience as mothers set us apart from many of our college peers who were seeking a more traditional student life. Our conversations centered around the joys and challenges of parenthood, and our friendship became a treasured source of support. Peppi's husband, Steve, a state trooper with a sharp, dry sense of humor, added another dimension to our friendship. Steve was the first police officer I knew personally.

I can't recall ever confiding in Peppi about my husband, save for the fact that he remained unemployed and was not someone I could entrust with our daughter.

Around the time our daughter turned four, I gifted Megan a pet bunny for Easter. One ordinary day, when I returned home from school, I stopped by to feed her bunny on my way into the house, only to find it lifeless, its cage having collapsed on top of it. The shock was overwhelming, and I immediately shielded my daughter from the distressing sight. With no cell phones available at the time, I placed Megan in the car and tried to flee. My husband claimed that the pet's death was an accident and then he blocked the driveway with his vehicle so that we could not leave. Fearful of running out of gas, I parked my car and took my daughter, retreating into the only bedroom to hide.

It was a night etched in my memory as one of the most terrifying I'd ever experienced. The night unfolded with his eventual unconsciousness, which was my opportunity to escape, taking with me only what I could fit into two bags. Rushing to a pay phone, I dialed Peppi's number and implored her for help. I had reached a breaking point and asked for what I desperately needed. Little did I know that this act of asking for help would prove to be transformative—a testament to the life-altering power of seeking assistance. The subsequent chain of events set in motion by my initial ask included reaching out to my parents, switching my daughter's daycare, and informing the campus police of my safety needs. Steve accompanied me to the courthouse, guiding me through the steps required to obtain a protective order. My parents arrived to provide a place for my daughter to hide. This experience ignited two profound transformations within me: the newfound courage to vocalize my needs and an unyielding passion for the workings of the criminal justice system.

Decades later, as I reflected on that pivotal chapter of my life, it dawned on me that Steve was, in fact, my very first mentor. At the time, I didn't fully grasp the significance of his guidance. It wasn't until a student, years later, posed the question of how my passion for investigations had ignited that I delved deep into my memories and, to my surprise, unearthed the profound influence that Steve had on my life's trajectory. He became an embodiment of not only how to treat one's family with respect and kindness but he also became a living testament to the remarkable impact police officers can have on someone's life. Law enforcement professionals often step into people's darkest moments, altering the course of their existence for a lifetime. A revelation that set the stage for my future journey into the world of criminal justice, that was not revealed until much later in my journey.

One of the best ways to describe mentorship is to understand what a mentor is not. A mentor is not a motivator, a mentor is not a teacher, a mentor is not a cheerleader; a mentor is a two-way relationship where one person sees in you perhaps something you cannot fully see in yourself and is willing to challenge you to take the action necessary to grow. This growth may be extremely uncomfortable for both the mentor and the mentee. The first step: the decision to seek guidance, to ask for help, to invite a mentor into your life. Here are several actionable steps to prepare you for identifying and initiating this process of mentorship:

1. **Self-Reflection:** Start by reflecting on your goals, dreams, and areas where you seek growth. What specific knowledge, skills, or experiences are you looking to gain? Clarifying your needs and objectives will help you identify the right mentor. You cannot ask for directions if you don't know where you are going!

2. **Define Your Ideal Mentor:** Envision the qualities, expertise, and personality traits you desire in a mentor. Consider factors like their experience, communication style, and compatibility with your goals and values. Write down areas in your life where you have seen dramatic progress; who were the people involved in that change?

3. **Network and Research:** Actively engage with your network and seek recommendations for potential mentors. Attend events, conferences, and seminars related to your field of interest. Additionally, tap into

online platforms, such as LinkedIn, to identify individuals who align with your mentorship needs.

4. **Reach Out:** Once you've identified a potential mentor, don't hesitate to reach out. Craft a personalized message expressing your admiration for their work and a genuine interest in learning from their experiences. Highlight how their guidance can align with your goals.

5. **Be Respectful of Their Time:** Understand that mentors are often busy professionals. Respect their time and availability and be concise and specific when requesting their guidance. A well-prepared request demonstrates your commitment and sincerity.

6. **Build the Relationship:** As the mentorship journey commences, focus on building a genuine, reciprocal relationship. Engage in meaningful conversations, actively listen to their advice, and be open to their feedback.

7. **Set Clear Goals:** Establish clear and realistic goals for your mentorship journey. What do you hope to achieve through this relationship? Share your objectives with your mentor, allowing them to better guide you.

8. **Set Mentor–Mentee Deliverables**: As your mentorship progresses, work together to define and track specific deliverables or outcomes. What should both you and your mentor expect from this partnership? These could include achieving certain milestones, improving particular skills, or creating a project together. By setting clear deliverables, you ensure that the mentorship remains purpose-driven and results-oriented, benefiting both you and your mentor.

9. **Show Gratitude:** Express your gratitude throughout the mentorship journey. Acknowledge the impact of their guidance, share your successes, and be appreciative of their time and insights.

Remember, mentorship is a two-way street. While you seek guidance and knowledge, you also have the opportunity to give back through your dedication, curiosity, and the impact of your future successes. The journey begins with that first step: asking for what you need and embracing the guidance of a mentor. We will outline more of this process as the chapters unfold.

The path I walked was filled with shadows, but the presence of mentors ensured I never lost sight of the light within me. Throughout this book, please keep in mind that I have an outstanding family, many spectacular teachers, and fabulous friends who have always had my back. I don't want to diminish their contribution to my successes; this book's aim is narrowly focused on the impact of mentorship exclusively. In this book, I aim to reveal how the nine powers of mentorship can help you realize the dreams that have been locked away. The mentorship process is entirely different from your life support system; often mentors are chosen for a stage of your life, or a specific career goal, and could only be in your life for a specified finite period of time.

Mentors can become friends; they might also become coaches or other forms of support throughout your life. My plan in this book is to attempt to stay focused on the transformative power of a more formal mentor relationship. Many of the benefits of this relationship come from progress tracking. If you want to monitor your success in any aspect of your life, science shows that tracking actions tends to increase the probability of reaching them.

In life, *asking* emerges as one of nine intricate tumblers within the lock of our dreams. Each tumbler is a unique facet of our journey, requiring precise alignment. Picture, if you will, the dream as a chamber sealed by this lock, waiting to be unveiled.

The mentor, like a masterful key, is the catalyst that begins to turn the tumblers, instilling a sense of direction and purpose. But the door will not yield until all nine tumblers align. The first step is to learn to ask for guidance, for support, for what we need. It is then that the key begins to find its way through the labyrinth of tumblers, and the dream, like a long-lost treasure, is finally unlocked, revealing the brilliance waiting within. This book is the journey, the guide, and the means to align your tumblers, unlock your dreams, and embrace the profound power of the ask.

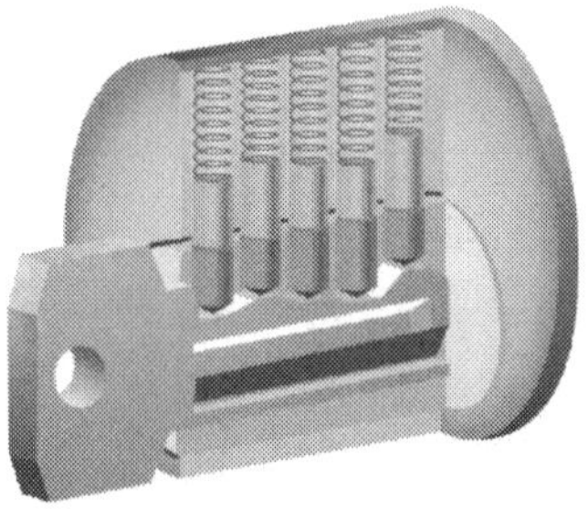

https://en.wikipedia.org/wiki/File:Pin_tumbler_with_key.svg#filelinks

"Mentoring is not about making people like you, but about helping them become the best version of themselves." ***—David Stoddard***

Get a FREE Copy of the 12-week Mentee Meeting Agenda to Facilitate Mentor–Mentee Meetings Here:

To Get Your Free Resources:

SCAN ME!

Steven A. Coppinger is now retired and writes amazing historical books about law enforcement and his family. Scan the below QR code to find his author page:

-... .-. . .- -.- .. -. --. / .- -. -.. / . -. - . .-. .. -. --.

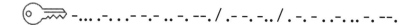

If you are interested in delving into the science behind the power of the ask, there are several aspects ripe for research. Decision-making, emotional intelligence, perception, and problem-solving are a few of the key areas that shed psychological insight into making successful choices.

Understanding the intricacies of the decision-making process is instrumental in enhancing both career progression and mentor relationships. In a professional context, decision-making often shapes the trajectory of one's career. Knowing more about this process allows individuals to make informed, strategic choices that align with their goals and values. It promotes the ability to assess risks, weigh options, and adapt to changing circumstances—crucial skills in a dynamic work environment.

Moreover, in mentor relationships, awareness of decision-making psychology fosters effective communication. Mentors can guide mentees in navigating complex choices, impart insight into potential biases, and encourage a thoughtful approach. For mentees, this knowledge enables them to make decisions that align with their long-term aspirations and values. It also contributes to the development of a resilient mindset, crucial for weathering challenges and setbacks in a career journey.

Social psychology highlights the impact of social norms, peer influence, and cultural factors on decision-making. Behavioral economics examines how biases and heuristics can lead to deviations from rational decision-making models. The psychological aspects of decision-making are multifaceted, encompassing risk aversion, loss aversion, and the role of intuition.

This chapter explores the psychology behind the reluctance people often feel when seeking help and the transformative impact of overcoming this hesitation. The aversion to asking for help often stems from concerns about vulnerability, fear of judgment, or a desire to appear self-sufficient. However, understanding the psychological dynamics at play reveals that seeking help is not a sign of weakness but rather a demonstration of strength and self-awareness. It signifies a proactive approach to personal and professional growth. There are numerous benefits to seeking help in the form of mentorship, it provides valuable insights, accelerates skill development, and opens doors to new opportunities. By delving into the psychology of overcoming the reluctance to ask for help, you can embrace the transformative power of seeking guidance, recognizing it as a catalyst for successful career progression and personal fulfillment.

My goal is to make this book a quick read, to get you in a position to take action as fast as possible. To achieve this, I am not going to cite tons of resources or technical jargon. I will end each chapter with several key ideas and places where you can grab some science behind the power. When searching for why, asking for help can be monumentally powerful. You can find websites and platforms like Psychology Today, TED Talks, and online courses on platforms like Coursera or Udemy that often feature content related to communication skills and assertiveness. I also recommend a book by Adam Grant titled *Give and Take: A Revolutionary Approach to Success.*

CHAPTER 2

The Power of Yes

Lafayette Lawson, The World Welterweight Kickboxing Champion

Leave Everything to Chance . . . As I was finishing up my bachelor's degree in business, I attended a career fair on campus. My life was still in chaos due to having to hide from my husband for our safety. I felt both excited and terrified about the unknowns of our future. In this mindset, I jumped at the first job offer—to work for Snoopy at MetLife selling life insurance. To summarize this experience, selling life insurance in your midtwenties is a complete disaster, not to say that someone couldn't be successful in this environment, but I was struggling.

My income was set up as a "draw," and my manager left due to a serious illness. After a few months of selling insurance to my family, the future grew increasingly bleak. It seemed that older couples did not want to talk about dying with a "kid," and my peer groups didn't care to talk about dying at all. Imagine the paradox. It came to the point where I was making cold calls in the yellow pages of the phone book. After numerous no responses, I called a tae kwon do studio and asked for the owner/manager. Mr. Lawson stated that he was the owner, so I proceeded with my sales message, and to my surprise, Lafayette said yes, and we set a 2 p.m. appointment that same day. I excitedly gathered my sales gear and planned to close a much-needed sale. Lean in, this is where this story gets good.

I arrived ten minutes early with my briefcase and strategy in hand. I walked through the front door and almost bumped into Lafayette. Remember, I know nothing about this business owner other than he said yes to my offer to talk about life insurance. Who I bumped into was a tall, handsome, muscular stranger in a tracksuit with a million-dollar smile. When he introduced himself, and I did the same, he said, "Hey, I forgot I have another appointment across town. Can you ride with me while we discuss life insurance?" If this were a movie, you would now hear the creepy Law & Order danger music. But I said yes. Without hesitation, I hopped into a stranger's car, and this divine selection in the phone book and singular decision to say yes began a cherished friendship and career trajectory that has brought me where I am today.

The MetLife training manual never brought up mobile appointments. Ironically, years later when I was in real estate, I pleaded with realtors *not* to get into cars with strangers or go to houses without the buyer coming by the office first, but thank goodness I wasn't a trained security professional at the time this opportunity happened. I also didn't know that getting a kickboxing champion life insurance was not something that underwriters wanted to do; seems it was too "risky" as a profession. The good news is that I was able to prove that Lafayette was not only in better physical shape than most candidates but the fact that he had to seek regular physicals before fights made him more likely to find any illness early as compared to the male population at his same age, who rarely went to preventive doctor visits.

That fateful yes echoed with the power to shape my journey. I had jumped into a stranger's car, putting aside all caution, and from that bold choice, an extraordinary mentorship was born. I met Lafayette's friends, one of whom became my private investigator business partner. Our children had birthdays on the same day two years apart. We became family. Many of my closest friends to this day (and several key future mentorships) started from knowing Lafayette. What began as a conversation about life insurance evolved into a lifetime of blessings that would guide my career and instill in me the strength to embrace the unknown. Saying yes to Lafayette unlocked doors I never knew existed.

This unique mentorship demonstrated the profound influence that comes from taking risks and following your instincts. As my career unfolded, I would continue to face choices where saying yes or no could dictate my path. With the wisdom I gained from this encounter, I found the confidence to make bold decisions, often against the odds. My mentor Lafayette, a champion in the ring, became a champion in my career journey. Together, we proved that life's most significant opportunities often arise when you're willing to take that leap of faith.

Mentorship, like the yes that began this chapter, is a transformative force. It opens doors, offers guidance, and pushes you to venture beyond your comfort zone. The power of mentorship is not merely about learning from others but about growing together. So, as you embark on your career path, remember the lesson of this chapter: sometimes, you must say yes when you're presented with an opportunity, no matter how unusual or unexpected it may seem. Your career, like mine, could be forever transformed by the magic of mentorship and the power of saying yes.

"True mentors have this unique ability to pick up vibes that everyone else misses from within you." ***—Ahmad R. Kazi***

Scan below to get your free quiz: "How Afraid of Change Am I?"

To Get Your Free Resources:

SCAN ME!

Mr. Lawson is currently writing two different books about the people he has met while he continues to be an inspirational personal trainer, promoter, and movie writer. We are racing to see who can get our book published first. See you at the finish line, Brother!

-... .-. . .- -.- .. -. --. / .- -. -.. / . -. - . .-. .. -. --.

There are psychological barriers that often underlie the reluctance to embrace new opportunities or step outside one's comfort zone. This hesitancy is intricately linked to the innate human resistance to change, rooted in a primal instinct for safety and familiarity. The psychological comfort derived from the known and routine creates a resistance to the unknown, even if it holds the potential for growth and advancement. Fear of failure, a natural human apprehension, also plays a significant role, as individuals grapple with the prospect of stepping into uncharted territory. Unraveling these psychological barriers reveals the complex interplay of risk aversion, fear of the unfamiliar, and the comfort derived from the status quo. If you find yourself especially risk-averse, perhaps you can seek to explore strategies to overcome these psychological hurdles. I recommend the book, *Think Again* by Adam Grant as a fantastic resource for growth.

As we embark on a journey of introspection and discovery, unravel the cognitive knots that may hinder your ascent and embrace the transformative potential that mentorship brings to those who dare to recognize the power of humility and the strength it takes to seek guidance. Below is a table outlining nine common barriers to change along with corresponding solutions:

Barrier to Change	Solution
Fear of the Unknown	Encourage a growth mindset; focus on potential benefits of change; gather information to reduce uncertainty; take small steps toward change.
Comfort Zone Resistance	Recognize the value of stepping outside comfort zones; challenge limiting beliefs; seek support from mentors or peers; set achievable goals to gradually expand comfort zones.
Lack of Confidence	Build self-esteem through positive affirmations and self-care practices; seek feedback and validation from supportive individuals; focus on past successes and strengths.
Overwhelm and Stress	Break down change into manageable tasks; prioritize and delegate responsibilities; practice stress management techniques such as mindfulness or exercise.
Attachment to Mediocrity	Reflect on the costs of maintaining the status quo; visualize potential benefits of change; seek inspiration from others who have successfully embraced change.

Fear of Failure	Embrace a growth mindset; reframe failures as opportunities for learning and growth; set realistic expectations and celebrate progress.
Lack of Resources	Identify available resources and leverage them creatively; seek assistance from mentors, peers, or professional networks; explore alternative solutions and approaches.
Resistance to Authority	Foster open communication and dialogue; provide rationale and context for change initiatives; involve stakeholders in decision-making processes; address concerns and seek a consensus.
Perceived Risk	Conduct thorough risk assessments; develop contingency plans; communicate clear expectations and potential benefits of change; provide support and training to mitigate risks.

Addressing these barriers to change can help you overcome resistance and embrace new opportunities with a positive mindset. Pick one of the above barriers that you recognized in yourself and search for a quick YouTube video or podcast where you can spend fifteen minutes working toward a nimbler decision-making outlook.

CHAPTER 3

The Power of Books

Arthur Paholke, The Father of Forensic Locksmithing

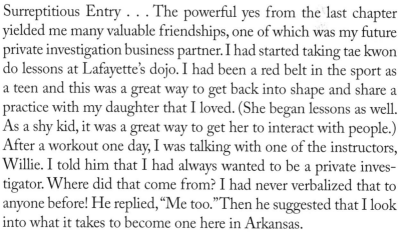

Surreptitious Entry . . . The powerful yes from the last chapter yielded me many valuable friendships, one of which was my future private investigation business partner. I had started taking tae kwon do lessons at Lafayette's dojo. I had been a red belt in the sport as a teen and this was a great way to get back into shape and share a practice with my daughter that I loved. (She began lessons as well. As a shy kid, it was a great way to get her to interact with people.) After a workout one day, I was talking with one of the instructors, Willie. I told him that I had always wanted to be a private investigator. Where did that come from? I had never verbalized that to anyone before! He replied, "Me too." Then he suggested that I look into what it takes to become one here in Arkansas.

Little did he know that research is one of my superpowers. I did not know it at that time, but I have since been clinically diagnosed with attention deficit disorder (ADD). Despite the many manifestations of this disorder, in my twenties and thirties, it worked as an asset for me. To be able to jump into alternative aspects of focus at a moment's notice and the need for hyper-organization made it appear that I was a multitasking master (ironically what at this very moment is making writing this book a tremendously difficult undertaking, in my fifties).

The next class, two days later, I had what I would now consider an entire business plan. From legal requirements to enrollment at the training academy to our first five-year earnings and goal projections. This shocked and confused him, but to make a very long story short, we opened our successful six-year private investigation business later that year.

Although I undoubtedly learned tons from this partnership, it is not considered a mentorship as we were both learning a new skill/career together. My partner had a full-time job, and the majority of the business details fell under my responsibility. I will forgo all the details about other part-time jobs and the wild stories of being a single mom and a budding detective. Often it felt more like an *Inspector Gadget* episode than a 007 movie, but we were passionate about learning and grabbed every opportunity we could find to advance. As part of my partner's career as a delivery driver, he had many decades-long relationships with professionals. My next mentor was introduced to me by Willie, and to this day it is an honor to have experienced a relationship with Sgt. Arthur R. Paholke, Retired C.P.D.

I can still remember driving out to the Hot Springs Village to meet who I later learned to be the "Father of Forensic Locksmithing." Art's smile, when meeting him for the first time, was like a kid meeting Santa. What his small, round stature concealed was his brilliant, scientific crime-fighting mind that shined with every twinkle of his eye. Our first meeting he offered me a glass of scotch and invited me to his basement (again at this stage in my career I would advise against taking drinks from strangers and following them into basements, but my partner had known Art for over a decade, so I felt safe and was still extremely naïve).

I admit I thought the scotch tasted like moss, an opinion I still hold today (apologies to you scotch lovers). I spent many hours enthralled in hearing his tales of mob crime fighting back in Chicago. Art's recounts of his time as a U.S. Navy Veteran in WWII and Korea enthralled my budding intellect as I had not ever discussed historical military events. Art would tell me about a case, show me a resource, and quiz me about what I learned at the end of each of our visits together. Often, he would give me assignments to be completed before our next visit. Sometimes alone, sometimes with my daughter, we could go to Art's basement to learn.

Art was kind and giving to everyone he encountered. He always gave my daughter small coins and trinkets. Mentors are often a generous breed. The time and effort involved in pouring your expertise into a mentee is a profound gift. As one of the first projects, Art insisted I begin constructing my curriculum vitae (CV) to delineate my training and qualifications. Art prepared me to understand how it would be used in court to qualify me as an expert witness. He shared his extensive and monumental career with me. From a decorated veteran to one of the founding members of the Association of Firearms and Tool Mark Examiners (AFTE), he was a trainer at the Federal Bureau of Investigation (FBI), and even in retirement continued to train local law enforcement professionals.

As unique as my training with Art was, so was his basement. From his historical criminal justice tools to the walls that displayed Art's enormous vintage doorknob collection, everywhere I looked, I was fascinated. It makes perfect sense that the man who was said to be the first person in court to successfully testify that a tool mark could be tied to a specific crime—thereby convicting the suspect of *breaking and entering*.

Throughout the following year, I observed Art gift people he had just met with custom handmade doorknob pen holders.

Art designed these with duplicate doorknobs from his collection. I was always secretly jealous of this; I couldn't understand why he never made one for me. They were sparkly and pretty. I really wanted one to display on my office desk. Although I never got a doorknob, Art would often conclude our learning sessions by giving me a book related to the topic we had discussed, and he would always inscribe it.

Art had explained that surreptitious entry was the ability to enter and exit a location without being detected; it has always been such a delight to find that many of the mentoring treasures he bestowed to me would not be discovered until much later in my growth journey. It was decades later (after Art had passed away) that I realized the gifts he gave me were exponentially more special than the doorknob desk delights. The gifts of inscribed books themselves are now among my most prized possessions. In addition to that, the gift of learning to research and the power of books has undoubtedly shaped my life beyond comprehension.

I was never an avid reader and only skimmed books in college. Truth be told, I'm still not an avid reader, I struggle to concentrate and focus when reading. I have learned that audiobooks are better for me. Find what works for your mind and your specific situation, it's to be celebrated that every journey is unique.

Expect your journey with your mentor to have aspects that you won't understand until your journey matures. This underscores the intricate dynamics of a mentorship journey, likening it to the pages of a book where many chapters remain unread and unknown. The mentee embarks on a journey with a mentor, yet the twists and turns and the challenges and triumphs that lie ahead are often veiled in uncertainty.

This emphasizes the importance of cultivating a deep understanding and trust in this journey. Much like turning the pages of a book, the mentee must surrender to the unfolding narrative, recognizing that the mentor's guidance, though at times unforeseeable, holds the key to unlocking valuable lessons and experiences. Trusting the process becomes a psychological anchor, allowing the mentee to glean maximum value from the mentorship journey, even in the face of the unknown.

"Our chief want in life is somebody who will make us do what we can." **—Ralph Waldo Emerson**

Scan below to get a copy of my CV checklist:

To Get Your Free Resources:

SCAN ME!

-... .-. . .- -.- .. -. --. / .- -. -.. / . -. - . .-. .. -. --.

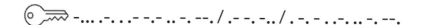

Engaging with books yields myriad cognitive, emotional, and social advantages, as acknowledged by psychology. On a cognitive level, reading stimulates various regions of the brain, enhancing neural connectivity and mental function. Stress reduction is a notable psychological benefit, as reading offers a form of escapism and relaxation. The development of empathy is facilitated through character identification and narrative transportation, contributing to enhanced emotional intelligence.

Furthermore, reading has been associated with improved mental health, acting as both a stress reducer and a coping mechanism. The expansion of knowledge and vocabulary is a cognitive boon, while increased focus and attentional skills are fostered by the sustained concentration required for reading. The social benefits include shared experiences and cultural understanding through literary exploration. Importantly, the power of reading extends to professional success, as it cultivates cognitive growth, resilience, and a broader life perspective. Exposure to diverse ideas and narratives enhances creativity and problem-solving skills, contributing to a well-rounded and adaptable mindset conducive to career advancement.

Reading becomes a powerful tool for acquiring new skills, gaining insights into industry trends, and staying abreast of evolving business landscapes. It equips individuals with valuable tools for navigating the complexities of their professional journeys. Science reveals that individuals who engage with nonfiction literature are better equipped to navigate challenges, make informed decisions, and innovate within their professional domains. There are various alternatives to reading printed books that have gained popularity. Below are some alternatives to printed books or different ways to engage with the power of books:

1. **E-books:** Electronic books, or e-books, can be read on e-readers, tablets, or smartphones. Platforms like Kindle, Nook, and Apple Books offer a vast selection of digital books.

2. **Audiobooks:** Audiobooks provide a listening experience, allowing people to "read" books while on the go. Services like Audible and Librivox offer a wide range of audiobooks.

3. **Digital Libraries:** Many libraries now offer digital lending services. Users can borrow and read e-books and audiobooks through platforms like OverDrive, Libby, or Hoopla using their library memberships.

4. **Book Subscription Services:** Platforms like Scribd and Kindle Unlimited offer subscription-based access to a vast library of e-books, audiobooks, and sometimes magazines.

5. **Podcasts:** While not a direct substitute for books, podcasts cover various topics and often include in-depth discussions and interviews that can be intellectually stimulating.

6. **Online Articles and Blogs:** For shorter reads, online articles and blogs are readily available on platforms like Medium, offering a wealth of information and opinions.
7. **Book Summaries:** Platforms like Blinkist and READINGRAPHICS provide condensed versions of nonfiction books, summarizing key insights for those looking for a quicker way to grasp the main ideas.
8. **Interactive Reading Apps:** Some platforms, like Goodreads, provide a space for readers to discover new books, track their reading progress, and engage in discussions with other readers.
9. **Book Clubs and Online Communities:** Joining a book club, whether in person or online, provides an engaging way to discuss and share thoughts on books.

To ensure you are retaining the power you are getting from books, we must talk about the forgetting curve. The forgetting curve, introduced by German psychologist Hermann Ebbinghaus in the late nineteenth century, illustrates the phenomenon of how information is rapidly forgotten over time if not actively reinforced. Murre and Dros (2015) successfully replicated Ebbinghauss' classic study that reports learners tend to forget up to 50 percent of newly acquired information within the first hour and up to 70 percent within the first day, with the rate of forgetting gradually leveling off over time.[1] To minimize the effects of the forgetting curve and enhance long-term retention of the benefits of books, learners can employ strategies such as spaced repetition and active recall. Spaced repetition involves reviewing material at intervals spaced out over time, allowing for more effective encoding and retention.

---

1 Jaap M. J. Murre and Joeri Dros, "Replication and Analysis of Ebbinghaus' Forgetting Curve," PLoS ONE 10, no. 7 (2015): e0120644, https://doi.org/10.1371/journal. pone.0120644.

Many articles I read suggest reviewing material three times over three days. This is a great YouTube video that I share with my students each semester: Strategies to overcome the forgetting curve (https://youtu.be/F5yiBm4z26o). Active recall involves retrieving information from memory rather than simply re-reading or passively reviewing, which strengthens memory recall and retention.

Several respected authors and researchers have contributed to the understanding of memory and learning processes, including the following:

1. **Daniel Kahneman**: A Nobel Prize-winning psychologist known for his work on cognitive biases and decision-making, Kahneman's book *Thinking, Fast and Slow* explores the dual systems of thinking and how they influence our judgments and behaviors.

2. **Barbara Oakley**: An educator and author of *A Mind for Numbers: How to Excel at Math and Science (Even If You Flunked Algebra)*, Oakley discusses effective learning techniques, including strategies to combat the forgetting curve and improve memory retention.

3. **Benedict Carey**: In his book *How We Learn: The Surprising Truth About When, Where, and Why It Happens*, Carey explores the science of learning and memory, offering practical insights into optimizing learning and minimizing forgetting.

By understanding the principles of the forgetting curve and implementing effective learning strategies advocated by respected authors in the field, you can enhance your retention of valuable insights and knowledge gleaned from books (or training), ensuring a more enduring impact on your personal and professional development.

CHAPTER 4

The Power of Certification

Raffaele Di Giorgio, The Protector

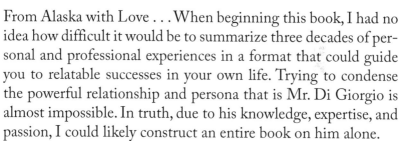

From Alaska with Love . . . When beginning this book, I had no idea how difficult it would be to summarize three decades of personal and professional experiences in a format that could guide you to relatable successes in your own life. Trying to condense the powerful relationship and persona that is Mr. Di Giorgio is almost impossible. In truth, due to his knowledge, expertise, and passion, I could likely construct an entire book on him alone.

Our meeting was like things that literal movies are made of. You see, Lafayette had written a movie that he was filming in Hot Springs, Arkansas (*The Color of a Dream*). My rottweiler, Rocky, had a part in the movie. I arrived at the given location to find what I could best describe as a huge, scary bouncer securing the door. (Later I found he owned the establishment.) I didn't think he would mind me describing my first impression of him as every "Italian from New Jersey" stereotype that I had in my very sheltered small-town existence. When I approached him, the arms-crossed, tough-guy protector turned into a jovial smiling guy exclaiming that I "gotta see his babies." He reached for his wallet, and to my amusement, he showed me a photo of his two rottweilers.

I still laugh out loud recalling this meeting, I remember thinking, *Who is this guy and why would I want to see his kids?* However, I was delighted to see his gorgeous pups! We exchanged contact information because you never know when a private investigator might need to call an ex-cop from New Jersey. One of Raffaele's plethora of talents is follow-through. The very next week he set an appointment to come to my office and compare CVs. The fact that I even had a CV was due to the masterful mentorship from Art. To this day I still don't know what Raffaele saw in me; however, he immediately began to mentor me. As a bonus to this relationship, I got to develop a priceless friendship with his wonderful wife, Jeannie.

Learning from Raffaele is like drinking water from a firehose; you must keep up, suck it up, and move your ass! Mentally, physically, and emotionally you must execute. When the task seems too difficult or impossible, then you need to work harder, work smarter, and kick that task's ass. No days off, no time to postpone success—pivot from your mistakes and keep the forward momentum in focus.

In my journey, this mentor's passion for protection is not just a professional duty; it's a calling, a profound commitment to ensuring the safety and well-being of those under his care. Raffaele's paragon of protection and unwavering expertise is unparalleled. One unique aspect of working with Raffaele is not only the depth of his knowledge but the breadth of his experiences. A seasoned military veteran and police officer, he has traversed the globe, sharing his expertise and training individuals in the art of protection. The extent of his impact goes beyond what can be openly acknowledged, given the clandestine nature of many of his projects.

There are no words that I can use to describe having a mentor as ingenious as Raffaele. His proficiency is a mosaic of experiences that have sculpted him into an unmatched authority in many professional fields. His mentorship was not confined to the transfer of knowledge but extended to the imparting of a mindset—a mentality of watchfulness, preparedness, and an unwavering commitment to safeguarding the welfare of others. In sharing my fortuitous journey of working with Raffaele, my aim is to pass on the invaluable lessons and transformative experiences that have shaped my professional and personal path to you, the reader.

As I recount his expertise, it becomes evident that his mentorship is a beacon, casting light on the profound responsibility and honor that comes with being a protector in a world that requires vigilance. Personally, knowing that there are people like Raffaele who spend their lives protecting me, my family, and my country with little thanks even to the peril of their own lives fills my eyes with tears and soul with gratitude.

Raffaele shared with me a cornerstone of professional advancement: industry certifications. As the ever-evolving landscape of various industries demands specialized knowledge and expertise, certifications emerge as powerful badges of proficiency. These credentials not only validate one's skill set but also open doors to new opportunities and heights of success. He not only encouraged me to join ASIS International but also discussed how the acquisition of industry-recognized certifications would serve as a strategic investment in my career, enhancing credibility, expanding networks, and positioning me as a leader in the criminal justice field.

This is the point where the shit gets real; having a mentor will not (nor should not) be all sunshine and rainbows. Navigating changes and challenges is not for the faint of heart. As stated earlier, a mentor is not your cheerleader; they are someone who has volunteered to help you be the best you *in spite of yourself*! It is beneficial to remind yourself that you cannot know what you don't know. A point will come when you either don't agree with your mentor or you have given up on yourself, or perhaps you are just legitimately having a life crisis and—wait for it—your mentor infers (or outright tells you if they are Italian and from New Jersey) that they don't give a fuck!

Life can be hard. Horrific things happen to good people; innocent children are starved and molested daily. If you are having a bad day, you can go talk to a police officer, a soldier, or a parent in a children's hospital to get a large dose of perspective. One day I was having a "poor me, I'm broke and a single mom in a male-dominated industry, things are so hard" kind of day.

When I saw the caller ID, I was excited to answer a call from Raffaele as he and Jeannie had moved to Alaska and it had been a long absence since our last communication. I have still repressed the contents of this call; all I know is that the verbal thrashing that I received resulted in a sobbing session and a nosebleed. I remember Raffaele asking, "Hello, are you still there?" I answered between sobs, "I'm going to have to let you go because you've bloodied my nose, over the phone, all the way from Alaska."

Although Raffaele and I had nothing in writing established, I wouldn't change a single thing about our over two-decade relationship. We have traveled past the mentor–mentee relationship; we are now family. However, navigating the boundaries between mentor and mentee can be crucial for establishing a conducive and professional mentorship environment. Here are several suggestions you can include in your formal plan:

1. **Clear Communication:** Foster an open line of communication from the outset. Clearly define the goals, expectations, and limitations of the mentorship. Discuss preferred communication channels, frequency of meetings, and the nature of topics that are within the scope of the mentorship.

2. **Mutual Respect:** Emphasize the importance of mutual respect. Both mentor and mentee should acknowledge each other's perspectives, experiences, and time commitments. Respect for each other's boundaries is fundamental to a healthy mentorship relationship.

3. **Establish Goals and Boundaries:** Clearly outline the goals of the mentorship and the boundaries that should be respected. Discuss personal and professional boundaries to ensure a comfortable and respectful working relationship. Discuss how feedback will be given and received. Establish a framework for providing constructive criticism and encourage mentees to express their preferences for feedback. This ensures that feedback is constructive and well received.

4. **Confidentiality Agreement:** Encourage mentors and mentees to treat sensitive information shared during the mentorship with the utmost confidentiality. This builds trust and creates a safe space for open dialogue.

5. **Regular Check-Ins:** Schedule regular check-ins to assess the dynamics of the mentorship. This provides an opportunity for both parties to discuss any concerns, address potential issues, and make adjustments to the mentorship structure if needed.

6. **Professional Development Focus:** While personal topics may naturally arise, mentors and mentees strive to keep the discussions centered around professional growth to maintain a focused and purposeful mentorship.

7. **Time Boundaries:** Both mentors and mentees likely have other commitments, and setting realistic time expectations helps manage workload and ensures a sustainable mentorship relationship.

8. **Flexibility and Adaptability:** As the mentorship evolves, goals may shift and the mentorship dynamic may change. Encourage both parties to be adaptable and communicate openly about any adjustments needed.

9. **Exit Plan:** Clearly define the duration or milestones of the mentorship and establish a process for closure. This allows both mentor and mentee to reflect on the experience and evaluate its impact.

Find the leading certifications in your industry, join your field's industry community, and go for it! There are so many epic stories I could share about the rollercoaster ride that occurred in my journey to achieve the Triple Crown certification that I still hold. ASIS International is the world's leading membership organization for security management professionals (www.asisonline.org).

Their website uses these three words to describe what their board certifications demonstrate in the industry: credibility, influence, and opportunity. Thousands of professionals have earned a credential in one of these three that acknowledges their mastery of security principles and skills. When a practitioner holds all three of their certifications, it is touted as a Triple Crown. I joined ASIS as a member (thanks, Raff!) in 2007.

I successfully obtained my Certified Protection Professional (CPP) certification in April 2009. True to his nature, Raffaele congratulated me, said some very endearing supportive words, and then immediately asked when I was going to take the next one. Upon researching the remaining two certifications, I found that only approximately one hundred professionals had earned this trifecta worldwide, none of whom was a woman. I immediately set the mammoth goal to be the first female to obtain a Triple Crown.

The timeline of my mentors often overlapped, making a linear account of these experiences impossible. I will leave you in suspense about this goal until the conclusion is discussed in Chapter 6. I would be remiss if I didn't offer you an off-topic tip about your safety in this chapter dedicated to my "protector" mentor. Scan the QR code below to get a copy of my article, "Go Bag, Stay Bag, & Back-ups":

To Get Your Free Resources:

SCAN ME!

"The mediocre mentor tells. The good mentor explains. The superior mentor demonstrates. The greatest mentors inspire!" **—Lucia Ballas Traynor**

Scan the link below to go to Mr. Di Giorgio's author link. Even if you feel like these topics are not in your field, I would encourage you to think outside the box and get a copy. I think it will inspire you to consider your professional responsibilities in ways you cannot imagine.

-... .-. . .- -.- .. -. --. / .- -. -.. / . -. - . .-. .. -. --.

In the realm of mentorship, understanding the science behind neuroplasticity can be a game-changer for you. Neuroplasticity refers to the brain's remarkable ability to reorganize itself by forming new neural connections. When you are confronted with change, be it in mindset or approach, the brain undergoes a dynamic process of adaptation. New pathways are forged, and existing connections are strengthened, contributing to the rewiring of cognitive functions.

However, it's essential for you to recognize that the brain is not a passive bystander in this process. Brain cells actively monitor progress, both positive and negative, creating a feedback loop that influences behavior. This monitoring system can either keep individuals stuck in unproductive patterns or propel them toward success. It underscores the importance of cultivating a growth-oriented mindset, where setbacks are viewed as opportunities for learning and refinement, ultimately fostering a positive trajectory in the mentorship journey.

A tremendous opportunity lies in a mentee's ability to actively participate in shaping their brain's response to change. By embracing challenges and approaching mentorship with an openness to new ideas, mentees can harness the power of neuroplasticity to rewire their thinking patterns positively. This transformative process not only enhances professional development but also contributes to a broader mindset shift, setting the stage for sustained success in both personal and career endeavors. The brain's plasticity grants individuals the agency to deliberately influence their cognitive landscape, making every mentee a sculptor of their own neurological destiny.

In addition to understanding the science behind neuroplasticity and its role in your learning journey, it's essential to recognize the significance of professional certifications in fostering career growth and success. Professional certifications serve as tangible evidence of one's expertise and commitment to continuous learning and professional development. In today's competitive job market, where employers seek candidates with specialized skills and qualifications, holding relevant certifications can significantly enhance one's credibility and marketability. If you are running your own business, certifications can showcase your legitimacy in the field. Many people can purchase a website and state they have "expertise," but the industry standard organizations can certify it.

Moreover, earning certifications allows individuals to stand out in a crowded field of professionals by demonstrating their proficiency in specific areas of expertise. This differentiation can be especially valuable in industries where specialized knowledge and skills are highly sought after, such as information technology, healthcare, project management, and finance. By investing time and effort into obtaining certifications relevant to their field, mentees position themselves as leaders in their field, gaining more opportunities and increasing earning potential.

Furthermore, professional certifications provide mentees with a structured framework for learning and skill development, helping them acquire in-depth knowledge and practical skills necessary to excel in their respective fields. Whether it's mastering the latest technologies, staying abreast of industry best practices, or gaining recognition from peers and employers, certifications offer a pathway to professional growth and success.

Incorporating professional certifications into your learning journey can not only harness the principles of neuroplasticity to enhance their cognitive abilities but can also equip them with the credentials and expertise needed to thrive in today's competitive job market. Clients want to work with people who are proven to be knowledgeable; certification and credentialing can be that added assurance that you are a trusted expert.

CHAPTER 5

The Power of the Underdog

Vera Davis, The Longshot & Mark Burrier, The Fixer

Betting on a Winner . . . Both of these mentors are phenomenal professionals; they worked harder than most can even comprehend, climbing to the tops of their respective fields. True testaments to the power of the underdog, Vera and Mark (my grasshopper) taught me so much!

I met Vera (and her husband, Don) through my business partner. As a first-time small business owner, I had a lot to learn—and that was an understatement. In capturing the essence of Vera, I would describe her not in inches or pounds but in the sheer intensity of her energy, akin to the unstoppable force of a hurricane that reshapes everything in its path. It was as if, when she entered a room, a powerful gust of inspiration and determination followed, rearranging the atmosphere and leaving an unmistakable imprint on all who had the privilege of standing in her formidable presence. I would also describe her as kind and funny, yet able to tear your face off if she needed to. As my first female mentor, she strengthened me in ways that my previous mentors could not.

Vera was also in the exact field that I wanted to excel at. My other mentors had been in law enforcement, but she was in security and investigations. From this mentor, I gleaned profound lessons about navigating the intricate landscape of a male-dominated industry as a woman. She embodied strength not by emulating the traits of her male counterparts but by embracing her authentic self. Her guidance was a masterclass in wielding femininity as a unique asset, showcasing that power doesn't require conformity.

She demonstrated the art of standing firm in her convictions, speaking her truth, and leading with empathy—traits often undervalued but undeniably potent. She taught me about resilience, grace under pressure, and the art of breaking barriers without losing one's essence. As I absorbed these lessons, I realized that many might consider this mentor an underdog, but once you spent any time with her, you would quickly understand that she was instead a powerful force to be reckoned with.

Vera was vastly different from me; however, the alignment in gender and career specialty compounded my experiential learning. Having a mentor who shares similarities with you is crucial for a variety of reasons.

First, it enhances relatability, creating a deeper connection as your mentor can better understand the challenges and aspirations that stem from shared backgrounds or experiences. This relatability leads to a more effective mentorship, where advice is tailored to your specific circumstances.

A mentor with similar experiences provides practical solutions based on firsthand knowledge, addressing challenges you may encounter along your journey. Additionally, shared cultural backgrounds foster a deeper understanding of industry nuances, enhancing your ability to navigate professional obstacles.

Trust, a fundamental element of mentorship, is often built more easily when your mentor has walked a similar path, fostering a strong and supportive relationship. Moreover, a mentor who mirrors your background can serve as a powerful source of inspiration, demonstrating that success is achievable for someone with shared characteristics.

Last, the mentor's network, particularly if it aligns with your background, can open doors to relevant opportunities within your community or industry.

Vera's approach to mentoring was very holistic; she wanted to see success in every aspect of my life. What we now call "work-life balance" was a new concept to me. Vera was a giving mentor—with her knowledge of the industry but also with actual gifts. As my success grew, she bought me milestone presents that I still treasure. Vera shared her wisdom about relationships, family life, religion, politics, health, and wealth. We laughed; humor was a unique way that Vera taught me about serious topics without them becoming overwhelming and depressing. Vera was the first mentor to talk frankly with me about the importance of taking care of your mental health in your success. She pointed out that sometimes if you are stuck the answer is to talk to your doctor about it. She furthermore said it is not something that you should ever be ashamed about, life is hard. She said there are times in your life that medical help might be necessary to get you over a rough patch.

I'll take the liberty here to say if you are struggling with physical or mental health struggles, you are worthy of assistance. In the journey toward success, it's crucial to prioritize your well-being. If you find yourself grappling with physical or mental health challenges, remember that seeking support is not a sign of weakness but a testament to your strength and self-awareness. Reach out to friends, family, or professionals who can offer guidance and understanding. Additionally, national resources like the National Helpline (1-800-662-HELP) provide confidential assistance for substance abuse and mental health issues.

Remember, taking care of yourself is an essential step on the path to achieving your goals.

While having a mentor with similarities offers these advantages, it's equally important to recognize the value of diversity in mentorship, which we will discuss further in Chapter 8, as exposure to various perspectives enriches your understanding of the professional landscape. Balancing mentors who share your experiences with those who bring diversity ensures a well-rounded and comprehensive mentorship experience.

Throughout your career progression, you are likely to have dips, curves, and perhaps even times when you take a detour. I had one such career divergence. I had grown weary of the chaotic lifestyle that surrounded the private investigation field in such a small market. Corporate investigative work was hard to secure, and marital/family cases were emotionally draining. The work was also physically draining, I logged over 79,000 miles on my vehicle in eighteen months. We investigated cheaters, thieves, liars, people sleeping with their cousins, preachers having affairs, and a disheartening amount of child abuse and neglect. There were weekly death threats on the office voicemail. After my appearance in court, it was somehow my fault that the drug abuser got their children removed from their residence. I needed to take a break and pivot my focus on raising my daughter, as she was now a tween.

Perhaps this is where you find yourself, in a season of change. This could involve taking a break, pursuing a different field, or engaging in activities that are not directly aligned with your initial career trajectory. It's a shift away from the conventional path, and individuals often use this time for personal growth, skill development, or exploring new interests before returning to their original career path or charting a new path. Like me, you might need a break.

During this pivot, I wanted to move closer to my sister to be involved in my brand-new nephew's life. Upon relocating, I took the time to explore a career I had always been interested in: real estate. Since my cassette-listening, infomercial-watching days, I have always been a huge Tony Robbins fan. His accounts of real estate success seemed within my grasp.

I honestly cannot remember how I found Century 21 Dunaway & Hart, but Pete Hart was a powerhouse. She was a broker with a passion for real estate, helping people, and for her family. It was an honor to work for her, and the fellow agents there were some of the finest people I've ever worked with. This is where the story of my next mentor unfolds.

We are over halfway through this book now, so I feel I can share a secret with you: I'm not the greatest salesperson. There I said it. I'm passionate about what I am doing, I love helping people, I am a raging extrovert and have no fear talking about or to anyone—but I also can admit I lack the one key attribute to be a tremendous salesperson.

Over the years I've observed extremely successful people in sales. The one thing they have in common is that to their core they 100 percent believe that if they don't sell their products or services, they are actually harming their customer. I've just never had that. I love sharing with people the benefits of projects I'm involved with. I can passionately explain why it is fabulous, sometimes to the point of genuine tears, I'm so moved. However, after we've shared our time together, I then feel that you should also be moved to take action on your own. What I'm describing is not slimy sales tactics, not tricking people into buying things they don't need or can't afford. It is a genuine gut-level momentum to help as many people as possible by sharing your expertise to match their needs to the product or service that you sell. This describes my next mentor, my wise grasshopper, Mark Burrier.

This term is usually used for the student in a learning position, but we were joking around and I said, "Oh wise grasshopper, what can your most gracious student learn from you today?" We laughed so hard for days about that and it just stuck!

There were many outstanding realtors at Century 21 Dunaway & Hart, but what drew me to Mark was the power of the underdog. Now some would find it hard to categorize Mark as an underdog: he's a winner, loves life, works harder than most, and loves to play hard as well. What I saw in him that was special was that when a real estate deal was going sideways, the other agents went to Mark to save it. You see, Mark is a fighter, like the underdog in a fight in the movies; there is a point before the triumphant music begins to play that you just don't know if it's possible to win.

Out of nowhere, Mark finds a unique way to make all the puzzle pieces fit, to force a win-win for all parties involved. It might be controversial as to why he is so successful, but if I had to pinpoint the most powerful lesson I learned from Mark, it is that he never says something is "their" job. If the other realtor doesn't know how to structure a short-sell, he does his work and their work too—all the time teaching them how to do it for themselves next time. Not in a micromanager style but instead as a micro mentor.

I have repeatedly observed Mark be the expert realtor, broker, contractor, inspector, mortgage lender, and first-time home buyer program instructor in order to get a couple successfully into their first home. Never in a boastful, condescending way, never complaining. In a teaching, mentoring, roll-up-your-sleeves-and-get-this-done-for-the-benefit-of-the-client kind of way. Mark is competitive; he does like to win, but he ensures that winning is always a team sport. That's why the chair across from his desk was frequently filled with people asking for his advice.

Another power that a successful underdog has is that they can recognize when someone is struggling, and they reach down to pull people up. Mark noted that over and over I would put in the effort, to do the "right things" but end up not closing the deal. This is yet another kind of invaluable mentor in your journey, totally different from my previous mentors.

Mark didn't try to teach me to sell. *Let that sink in.* A natural pattern that some mentor or coaching relationships take is that the mentor excels at a specific skill, and they then pass a part of that knowledge onto their mentee.

Mark instead saw the talents I already had and put me in the right spot to succeed. He offered me a salaried position on his team as a listing agent, then he taught me everything he knew about how to be a successful listing agent. He invested his time, he invested in innovative training programs, and he invested in me. My time being mentored by Mark was about so much more than real estate. When I felt it was time for me to move back into the criminal justice field, Mark was supportive. To this day he supports me in everything I do. He is a dear friend (as well as his wife, Belinda), and of course, he is my Realtor.

We make a living by what we get, but we make a life by what we give." ***—Winston Churchill***

To get a free copy of my article about how to use Google Keep as your second brain, scan below:

To Get Your Free Resources:

SCAN ME!

-... .-. . .- -.- .. -. --. / .- -. -.. / . -. - . .-. .. -. --.

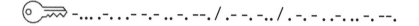

Although my two mentors above did *not* have this issue, I have repeatedly observed a roadblock to some very smart people when it comes to seeking mentorship. In the journey of personal and professional development, the Dunning-Kruger effect emerges as both a cautionary tale and a beacon of enlightenment. This psychological phenomenon, named after social psychologists David Dunning and Justin Kruger, illuminates the paradoxical tendency of individuals with low ability at a task to overestimate their competence. As a mentee, we might miss the cognitive blind spots that may lead individuals to believe they stand self-sufficient atop a mountain of expertise.

The underdog, in the context of the Dunning-Kruger effect, often finds themselves perched on the precipice of inflated confidence. The mentee after all is likely doing many things fantastically. They are blazing new trails; they are getting noticed.

These early successes can lead you to think you know everything. You don't need a mentor, because you mistakenly perceive your skills as more refined than they are, an optical illusion generated by a lack of metacognitive awareness. It's not a lack of intelligence that breeds this miscalculation but rather a deficit in recognizing one's shortcomings. The underdog is often exceptional in their area of expertise. This is why they stand out, why people are taking notice of their talents. This can sometimes lead to the mistake of extrapolating this to all areas of their knowledge and skills.

Mentorship, in its essence, becomes the compass that guides the underdog through the fog of overestimation. A mentor, with their seasoned perspective and unbiased insights, becomes the illuminating force that dispels the shadows of overconfidence. The Dunning-Kruger effect, while potentially veiling the need for mentorship, underscores the importance of humility—the acknowledgment that there is always room for growth and learning.

Seeking a mentor is not an admission of weakness but a proclamation of strength. It is the audacious step toward acknowledging the vast expanse of knowledge that awaits beyond the crest of one's current understanding. A mentor becomes the shaper of a reality check, gently steering the mentee away from the cliffs of overestimation toward the fertile valleys of continuous improvement.

CHAPTER 6

The Power of Organizations & Service

Craig Russell, The Professional & Eduardo Garcia, The Learner

Membership Has Its Privileges . . . There are times when a mentor gently nudges you in the way that you should walk, and there are times when they give you a commandment. In 2007, Raffaele said "You need to join ASIS" in a tone that I understood not to be a suggestion. Where Art began my CV-building journey, Raffaele emphasized the importance of building my network. Raffaele and I were geographically separated at this time, and he could not physically introduce me to other professionals in my area; that's where ASIS would become a valuable part of my success story.

Regardless of your career industry, there is likely an organization of like-minded people who gather to further the training, support, and mutual goals of the group. In the security industry, ASIS International is the predominant organization. I joined the national organization and then found the local chapter to attend a meeting. I showed up and to my delight found the group to be warm and welcoming. I explained that my mentor had advised me to join and that I was interested in their certification programs.

Since joining almost two decades ago, there has never been a time that this organization has not provided me with support and professional growth opportunities. From the local chapter to the members I've met across the globe, the one word that describes this group is *professional.* My next mentor, Craig Russell, personifies a professional. He is the Director of Public Safety at a private university and has held almost every leadership position in the ASIS organization that a volunteer can hold.

This was a clandestine mentorship; I didn't know it was going on when it first happened. Craig was always there leading from the front, facilitating growth for his team, his many colleagues, our organization, his university, the community, and his students. When I slowed down enough to notice, I recall Craig quietly, consistently promoting me, setting me up for success, and giving me opportunities to grow while always being there to support me. Never overlook the professional mentor in your circle, the one that everyone respects and who can quietly open doors for you and stand in the back clapping when you achieve the next milestone.

What makes this a mentorship instead of someone who likes and promotes you is the reciprocity element. When Craig unlocked the doors for me, I walked through and actively completed my part. I spoke at events, held certification trainings, and mentored new members. I observed how to be a leader in an organization and took action to emulate his success. In organizational settings, mentorship often takes on various forms, ranging from formal mentorship programs to informal relationships established between colleagues.

Do not overlook these informal mentorships. These mentorships can manifest organically through informal relationships formed between colleagues or within professional networks. In these instances, individuals may seek out mentors who possess specific skills or experiences relevant to their career aspirations. Informal mentorship relationships often develop through mutual respect, shared interests, and a willingness to learn from one another. Mentors in organizational settings may offer guidance on navigating workplace challenges, developing essential skills, and identifying opportunities for growth and advancement.

Furthermore, mentorship can extend beyond the boundaries of individual organizations to encompass broader service-oriented initiatives and professional networks. Engaging in volunteer work, participating in industry associations, or joining professional societies can provide mentees with access to a diverse range of mentors and opportunities for mentorship. By actively participating in service-oriented activities and professional communities, you can expand your networks, gain exposure to new perspectives, and develop valuable mentorship relationships that contribute to your personal and professional development.

I have a Doctor of Forensic Psychology at this very moment because of one such informal mentorship. There are countless friendships and relationships that I have formed with fellow ASIS members; one such member made a huge impact in my life, Ed Garcia. Ed noticed our mutual love of learning and almost immediately upon meeting me began to mentor me. He was an instructor at the University of Arkansas at Little Rock and also a member of ASIS International. We met at the local chapter meeting and discussed my goal of certification. He (like Craig) held the prestigious CPP (Certified Protection Professional) designation.

Every time I spent time with Ed, he had an article, a book, or a training program to share with me. Ed mentored me in how to develop training for my security staff as well as chapter events. We planned community service initiatives, and one day Ed asked me, "Have you ever thought about going back to school to get your master's degree?" I confided that I had always wanted to; my undergraduate degree was in business, but I longed to get my master's degree in criminal justice. After confessing my hidden desire, I then began to list the multitude of excuses why I could never do this. I didn't have the money, I didn't have the time, I didn't know how to even think about adding this task to my already busy sixty-to-eighty-hour workweek. Had he forgotten that I'd completed my CPP but was on a mission to be the first female in the world to achieve a Triple Crown?

In addition to his dedication to service, Ed believes in the quote "*ancora imparo.*" He shared with me that *ancora imparo* is an Italian phrase attributed to Michelangelo. It translates to "I am still learning" in English. Michelangelo reportedly uttered these words toward the end of his life, reflecting his acknowledgment of the ongoing process of learning and self-improvement, even in old age. The phrase encapsulates the idea that learning is a lifelong journey and emphasizes the importance of humility, curiosity, and a growth mindset. Ed simply said, "How about you send me your CV and I'll forward it to our director, Dr. Parker."

This was the summer of 2010, and by August somehow, I had completed my student aid information, taken the entrance exam, and enrolled in the online master's degree program. To this day, I'm unclear how it happened. In this program, I learned how to apply the real-world experiences I had gained in my career to the principles that we were learning in criminology. I became a sought-after speaker, where organizations and associations asked me to come and speak on the powerful benefits of formal education and certification.

I had successfully achieved the PCI (Professional Certified Investigator) credential and was trying to make the time to study for the PSP (Physical Security Professional) when I read the announcement about a marvelous global female security practitioner who had obtained the Triple Crown. I relinquished the goal of being the first and decided I could now be the first in the US.

Work responsibilities, graduate school, and what little time I had for a personal life were all barriers to preparing for the PSP exam. I had a bit of the Dunning-Kruger effect occurring, I had passed two certifications, I bet I'm smart enough to just cram for the exam over the weekend and pass. Wrong. After the reality check, I thought I'd take a couple of weeks and take it again. Missed the passing score again! One day I read the notice about two other females in the States and another international female who had obtained the Triple Crown. I finally passed my PSP exam and became a Triple Crown recipient in 2014. (Craig was in the audience at the ASIS annual seminar for my awards ceremony.)

Mentorship and networking can function as force multipliers in various contexts, amplifying the impact and effectiveness of individuals and organizations. Here's how they can be utilized as force multipliers:

1. **Knowledge and Skill Sharing:** Through mentorship, experienced individuals share their expertise, knowledge, and skills with mentees. This transfer of knowledge not only benefits the mentee but also enhances the collective capabilities of the organization or community. Additionally, networking allows you to connect with others possessing diverse skills and expertise, enabling the exchange of ideas and best practices across different domains.

2. **Amplified Influence and Reach:** Mentors often have established networks and credibility within their respective fields. By mentoring others, they extend their influence and reach, creating a ripple effect as mentees gain knowledge, confidence, and opportunities. Similarly, networking expands one's sphere of influence by connecting you with a broader audience, allowing you to amplify their message, goals, and initiatives.

3. **Collaborative Problem-Solving:** Mentorship and networking facilitate collaborative problem-solving by bringing together individuals with diverse perspectives and experiences. Mentors can guide mentees in tackling complex challenges, offering insights and strategies informed by their own experiences. Networking enables you to tap into a vast pool of resources, expertise, and support, fostering collaborative efforts to address common issues or achieve shared goals.

4. **Career Advancement and Opportunities:** Mentorship and networking play pivotal roles in career advancement and professional development. Mentors can provide guidance, advice, and advocacy to help mentees navigate their career paths, seize opportunities, and overcome obstacles. Networking exposes you to potential career opportunities, job prospects, and professional connections, thereby expanding your options and possibilities for growth.

5. **Enhanced Learning and Adaptability:** Mentorship and networking foster a culture of continuous learning and adaptability. This personalized guidance, feedback, and learning opportunity accelerates your learning curve and skill development. Networking exposes you to new ideas, trends, and perspectives, encouraging you to stay informed, adaptable, and innovative in your approach, including shortcuts to best practices and technology hacks that can streamline your efficiency.

6. **Access to Funding and Resources:** Mentorship and networking can provide entrepreneurs and students with access to funding opportunities, investors, and essential resources needed to launch or grow their ventures. Mentors with industry connections can offer

introductions to potential investors, accelerators, and funding sources, while networking allows you to build relationships with stakeholders and partners who can provide financial support or access to critical resources you might not otherwise have access to at this stage in your journey.

7. **Validation and Market Insights:** Mentorship and networking offer entrepreneurs valuable validation and market insights for their business ideas and projects. Mentors with industry experience can provide feedback, validation, and market analysis to help entrepreneurs refine their business concepts, identify market gaps, and validate their value propositions. Networking enables you to connect with potential customers, industry experts, and mentors who can offer valuable insights, feedback, and market intelligence to inform their business strategies and decision-making.

8. **Personal and Professional Development:** Mentorship and networking contribute to the personal and professional development of entrepreneurs and students by providing them with guidance, support, and learning opportunities. Mentors can serve as role models, offering advice, encouragement, and mentorship tailored to the individual's goals, aspirations, and challenges. A mentoring relationship, traditionally viewed as more beneficial to the mentee, can indeed offer substantial benefits to the mentor, creating a mutually enriching dynamic. Mentees often bring fresh ideas and perspectives, challenging mentors to re-evaluate their own views and practices, which leads to innovative thinking and problem-solving. In today's rapidly changing world, mentees can introduce mentors to new technologies and cultural trends, facilitating a reverse mentoring process that

helps mentors stay relevant. The personal fulfillment derived from witnessing a mentee's growth, alongside the opportunity to refine leadership and coaching skills, enhances the mentor's own professional and personal development. Furthermore, mentoring allows mentors to expand their professional network through their mentee's contacts, enriching both parties' career opportunities. Mentors also have the unique opportunity to contribute to their industry's legacy by shaping emerging talents, thereby leaving a lasting impact. This, combined with the enhancement of organizational culture through the promotion of continuous learning, underscores the profound, reciprocal benefits of a well-balanced mentoring relationship

9. **Partnerships:** Mentorship and networking opens doors to career opportunities, partnerships, and collaborations that can accelerate the growth and success of entrepreneurs and students years beyond a traditional education. Mentors can provide career guidance, introductions to industry leaders, and opportunities for internships, job placements, and collaborative projects. Networking facilitates connections with potential collaborators, cofounders, and strategic partners who share complementary skills, resources, and visions, enabling you to forge mutually beneficial partnerships that drive innovation, growth, and impact in your ventures or academic pursuits.

Overall, mentorship and networking serve as force multipliers by leveraging collective knowledge, influence, resources, and collaboration to achieve greater impact, success, and resilience in personal and professional endeavors.

After I finished the master's program, I rolled straight into a PhD program because I was already used to the chaos of "doing it all" and I told my FBI study pal (Reid) that the next seven (yes, seven) years would pass whether we were working toward our doctorate or not so let's do it. (It took me almost ten but that's a different story!) He said he would be glad to call me "Dr." but he was never going to school again! Now he's making epic accomplishments in his career. Everyone's route is not the same. (I just hope he has me saved at "Dr." in his phone.)

To emphasize this exponential point, the instructors I had in my master's program (Dr. Mary Parker, Dr. David Montague, and Dr. Jim Golden) are now my colleagues at the university where I teach. My prior networking with them as a student provided a foundation where I felt confident to apply for my current teaching position. They had also witnessed my solid reputation of education as well as experience to expound upon; I wasn't just an electronic CV.

During the time I was working on my PhD, Raffaele wrote an open letter to the North American Bodyguard Association (NABA) congratulating me on the Triple Crown, which I still have attached to my CV. I am still extremely proud of each of my accomplishments.

Like intricate building blocks, each next step was built on the last. Not to say that there were no setbacks or sideroads. There were, as should be expected. During those rough times, my varied mentors provided a place for me to recenter myself and gain some much-needed perspective. I have no doubts that the unique culmination of mentors and experiences led me to exactly where I am today. From the random call in the back of the Yellow Pages to the writing of this book, each of these nine powerful mentor types continues to guide my success.

"A mentor is someone who allows you to see the hope inside yourself." ***—Oprah Winfrey***

Scan this QR code to subscribe to my LinkedIn newsletter:

-... .-. . .- -.- .. -. --./ .- -. -../ . -. - . .-. .. -. --.

The subtitle of this chapter, "Membership Has Its Privileges," came to mind as a throwback to a popular commercial for a credit card that used that slogan. When we embark on our journey as professionals or entrepreneurs, the concept of wealth can take center stage. It's not just about monetary success; it's also about the mindset we carry regarding wealth and our worthiness to attain it. Exploring the psychology behind wealth and addressing the limiting beliefs that may have been ingrained since childhood is especially crucial for solopreneurs to truly thrive in their business endeavors. Let's examine the power of early influences to decode any adult behaviors that might be holding you back.

As children, we absorb messages from our families about wealth, scarcity, and success. These early influences play a significant role in shaping our beliefs and attitudes toward money. If we grew up hearing phrases like "money doesn't grow on trees" or witnessing financial struggles, we may unknowingly internalize beliefs that money is scarce, unattainable, or inherently evil.

The echoes of our childhood experiences often reverberate into adulthood, shaping our perceptions and behaviors around wealth. These experiences can manifest in subtle yet telling ways, giving us clues into the presence of limiting beliefs:

1. **Fear of Taking Risks:** If you find yourself hesitating to invest in your business or take calculated risks, it might be linked to a childhood environment where financial decisions were regarded with caution or anxiety.
2. **Self-Sabotaging Behavior:** Procrastination, self-doubt, or setting lower goals than you're capable of achieving can be signs of a subconscious belief that you don't deserve success or that it's unattainable.
3. **Money Avoidance:** An aversion to discussing or managing money might stem from childhood memories of financial stress or conversations around scarcity that made you uncomfortable.
4. **Undervaluing Your Work:** If you consistently undercharge for your services or products, it could indicate an underlying belief that you shouldn't demand fair compensation for your expertise.
5. **Impulsive Spending:** Paradoxically, an ingrained scarcity mindset might lead to moments of impulsive spending when you believe you've finally earned some financial breathing room.
6. **Reluctance to Invest in Self:** Resisting investments in personal or professional development may reflect a deeply rooted belief that spending on growth is a luxury you can't afford.
7. **Equating Wealth with Guilt:** If achieving financial success evokes feelings of guilt or unworthiness, it's worth exploring whether these emotions trace back to early lessons about money's perceived negative effects.
8. **Avoiding Success Spotlight:** Shying away from recognition or visibility, despite your accomplishments, could indicate an unconscious fear that standing out

could lead to negative consequences. Conversely, constantly comparing yourself to others and feeling envious of their achievements may indicate an internalized belief that there's not enough success to go around.

9. **Beliefs about Hard Work:** The conviction that wealth can only be acquired through exhaustive labor may stem from childhood teachings about the virtue of hard work without considering other avenues to success.

Recognizing these adult behaviors can offer valuable insights into the subconscious beliefs that were ingrained in childhood. By identifying and addressing these patterns, you take a significant step toward breaking free from limiting beliefs and fostering a healthier relationship with wealth and success. Your mentor might help you recognize some thoughts that could need a bit of mindset overhaul.

Do you eat burnt toast? I once watched a Barbara Walters special where she was interviewing actress Teri Hatcher. Teri said her mother used to eat the accidentally burnt toast, which gave her the erroneous feeling that for her to get good things other people must have bad things. This statement impacted me, even some twenty years later, I often think about this imbalance occurring in my own life or when I notice it happening in other people around me. If an average loaf of bread has twenty-four slices, one slice of bread is just a bit over four cents. For someone to eat a burned piece is most often not a financial necessity; therefore, why would anyone eat it, and then moreover, why would they wear it like a badge of honor? I see times when I've done it in my own life: "No, no, honey, you have the good piece of toast, I'll eat the burned piece." Why? A better response could be, "We have lots of bread. No one must eat burnt toast, we can just make more."

CHAPTER 7

The Power of Action & Delegation

Allen Hardin, The Action Coach & Joshua Blockburger, The Master Delegator

Do the Damn Thing (Unless You Can Have Someone Else Do It) . . . These last four mentor stories are not in chronological order; it made more sense for me to align the powers in this order toward the conclusion. Allen Hardin has been a friend of mine for decades. We met as part of my close circle of ballroom-dancing friends who found each other when my daughter began competing in Dancesport at the age of fourteen. We were a motley crew of ages, backgrounds, occupations, and dance ability, but we were family. We lived life together, we traveled, we laughed, we cried, and we worked as hard as we could as fast as we could so we could all meet again the next day to share our love of music and movement. It was a glorious time. Fast-forward to a time when we were all working too hard, we seldom saw each other, and I think we were too busy to do enjoyable things. I know I wasn't taking time to manage my work-life balance. This went on for years. Then the world shut down.

I know the global pandemic of 2020–2022 affected everyone differently; for me, it was a debilitating time of isolation and despair. For an extroverted person who gets her source of energy from being around people, it quickly became a huge barrier to my daily wellness. Due to my underlying health issues, my doctor advised that I stay indoors and not even risk being around my family. I could write a book about how devastating this time was, but this is when an unexpected mentor showed up in my life. I don't even remember why or what started our conversation, but Allen asked if I was doing okay. I was honest and simply said no. He immediately jumped into action and used his skills as a certified life coach to remotely change the course of my downward spiral. I won't tell you what he did because you would need to hire him to find that out, but what I can tell you is that he taught me half of the seventh power—the power of action and delegation.

This sounds simplistic. Most people understand mentally that they need to take action to not only be successful at their goals but just to get out of bed each day. I've read countless books about the topic. However, what the mentorship with Allen taught me was that action is the most important part of the equation, not necessarily what the specific action was. To just "do the damn thing," planning and executing intentional, small, relentless action steps is the foundation where most success originates.

The commitment on his part to my success was epic; he spoke with me every day from 6:30–7:00 p.m. for four weeks (then weekly for four more weeks). I just looked back at my goal sheet from when we started working together and one was to finish my PhD and another was to publish my book (done and done). During this eight-week intensive training program, Allen grounded me mentally through routine and action. In the upcoming chapter, I will delve deeper into the remarkable advantages of receiving coaching. Without Allen, my statistics coach (thanks, Dr. Tom Granoff), and Tony Robbins, I truly doubt I would have successfully completed my PhD.

This brings me to the second half of this power, the art of delegation (or outsourcing). For every action, there is an equal yet opposite learning point. One of the key concepts to achieving great things is to know when not to act. To be a true team leader, you must invest in your team and then trust them to prosper. My membership in ASIS introduced me to one of the most prodigious minds and skilled delegators I have ever had the pleasure to know, Joshua Blockburger.

Getting to know Joshua is an astounding process, being mentored by him is invigorating. His breadth and depth of knowledge is amazing, but it is his passion for connecting with people that drew me to Joshua at our ASIS meetings. He was able to construct solutions to issues and projects that were unique and beneficial to all participants. It wasn't until I served on the local board with him at the chapter chair that I learned about the power of delegation. I had never worked alongside someone who was a skilled delegator. I think we have all likely been on the receiving end of a poor delegator: someone who delegates to side-step their responsibilities. This is not what I'm describing. When done properly, delegation makes the entire team more effective, and more successful.

Recognizing the strengths of his team members, Joshua carefully assessed each task and assigned responsibilities accordingly. Instead of micromanaging, he empowered his team by clearly communicating expectations, providing necessary resources, and offering support along the way. Throughout projects, Joshua remained accessible for guidance and feedback, fostering an open and collaborative environment. I always felt empowered to make decisions autonomously, knowing that Joshua trusted my judgment and supported my efforts. With a clear understanding of my role and the project's objectives, I enthusiastically embraced the challenge, pouring my energy and creativity into crafting impactful solutions.

Through our regular check-ins, Joshua mentored me through the progress and addressed any obstacles. His proactive approach ensured that I had the support and resources needed to overcome challenges and stay on track. I observed Joshua do this in many forms with many types of people. Through effective delegation, Joshua leads his team members to grow and thrive in their roles. By leveraging their individual strengths and fostering an environment of trust and collaboration, Joshua was able to get results that only a few leaders ever achieve.

Delegating does not come naturally to me; I mistakenly try to do it all myself. My time being mentored by Joshua taught me so much, and when I get overwhelmed, or a project is running off the rails, I often think, *What would Joshua do?*

"My job is not to be easy on people. My job is to take these great people we have and to push them and make them even better." ***—Steve Jobs***

Scan below to get your FREE action pack cards:

To Get Your Free Resources:

SCAN ME!

-... .-. . .- -.- .. -. --. / .- -. -.. / . -. - . .-. .. -. --.

Here are nine general benefits of delegation when expressed ethically and positively:

1. **Enhanced Productivity:** Delegation allows you to focus your time and energy on high-priority tasks that align with your strengths and expertise, leading to increased productivity and efficiency in achieving goals and objectives.

2. **Skill Development:** Delegating tasks provides opportunities for team members to develop new skills, gain valuable experience, and expand their capabilities, fostering their personal and professional growth.

3. **Empowerment and Motivation:** Delegation empowers others by entrusting them with responsibilities and decision-making authority, fostering a sense of ownership, pride, and motivation in their work, which can lead to higher levels of engagement and job satisfaction.

4. **Collaboration and Teamwork:** Delegation encourages collaboration and teamwork within the organization, as team members work together to accomplish shared goals and objectives, leveraging each other's strengths and expertise to achieve collective success.

5. **Time Management:** Delegation helps you effectively manage your time by prioritizing tasks and delegating less-critical or time-consuming activities to others, allowing you to focus on strategic initiatives and value-adding activities that drive business growth and innovation.

6. **Stress Reduction:** Delegating tasks alleviates the burden of excessive workload and responsibilities, reducing stress and burnout and promoting overall well-being and work-life balance.

7. **Business Scalability:** Delegation enables you to scale your operations and expand your capabilities by leveraging the expertise and resources of others, allowing you the time to take on larger projects, pursue new opportunities, and adapt to changing market demands effectively.

8. **Cost Efficiency:** Outsourcing can be a form of delegation. Outsourcing allows you to access specialized skills and resources at a lower cost compared to hiring in-house staff or conducting certain tasks internally. By gaining the expertise of external service providers, you can reduce operational expenses while maintaining high-quality standards and achieving cost savings in the long run.

9. **Focusing on Core Competencies:** Outsourcing non-core functions and repetitive tasks enables you to focus time, energy, and resources on core business activities that drive revenue growth, innovation, and competitive advantage. By entrusting peripheral tasks to external vendors, partners, or technology, you can streamline your operations, enhance strategic agility, and maintain a sharper focus on your unique value proposition and market differentiation.

By embracing delegation as a strategic tool for effective leadership and teamwork, you can unlock your full potential, achieve greater success, and create a positive and empowering work environment. Step into the power of delegation and find a mentor who can show you this rare skill.

CHAPTER 8

The Power of Diversity

Dr. Arielle Woodyard, The Life Coach

What You Desperately Need Is Sitting at the Next Table . . .
Once upon a time (I always wanted to write that in a book) I was at my PhD residency (think huge expo of thousands of students over multiple disciplines in a hotel venue taking different sessions of learning modules and advising meetings) and was utterly overwhelmed, frustrated, and overall downtrodden in spirit. This was my first of four required residencies, and each session that I completed throughout the day only led me to believe that I would never be successful in this endeavor. This session was specifically for the forensic psychology cohorts. I don't recall if she sat at my table or if I sat at her table, but like God's plan of picking names from the phone book, this table was where I was meant to be. I met a new friend who would later become my life coach, Arielle Woodyard. Immediately I was impressed; she was young, beautiful, gifted, driven, energetic, full of purpose, and had an infectious sense of humor.

This chapter is about the power of diversity. I've observed this power in two ways: active personal diversity and the benefits of diverse coaching (compensated and non-compensated). Arielle ended up filling two of those roles in my life. I was at a stage in my life where most of my friends were from my career or long-term friends. To be honest, I wasn't shopping for new "inner circle" friends. Don't get me wrong, I love meeting new people, and as an extrovert, I have an ever-expanding group of friends. I hope *you* are going to be my friend after reading this book! Arielle was younger than my daughter, didn't have any kids, lived on the other side of the country, and wasn't into ballroom dancing. On the surface we didn't have much to bond over besides the pesky PhD project. However, despite my grumpy close-minded attitude, we became fast friends. We began planning our next residency together.

The moral of this story is don't think your mentors or coaches have to look or be like you to have a wildly successful relationship. Ever since leaving the small town I grew up in, I've practiced "active diversity." This goes beyond mere acknowledgment of differences to actively fostering an inclusive environment that values and celebrates diversity in all its forms. Active diversity entails proactive efforts to promote equality, respect, and understanding among individuals from diverse backgrounds, including but not limited to race, ethnicity, gender, sexual orientation, age, religion, socioeconomic status, and abilities.

At its core, active diversity recognizes that diversity is not just a checkbox or a buzzword but an essential ingredient for innovation, creativity, and success in today's interconnected world. It involves cultivating a culture where everyone feels valued, respected, and empowered to contribute their unique perspectives and talents. This means actively challenging biases, stereotypes, and discrimination while promoting equity and inclusion. Although this is the core way I live my life, when I met Arielle, a tiny part of me felt I couldn't learn anything from her because I was old enough to be her mom! I am glad that this bias didn't last long because Arielle was a huge part of why (and how) I finished my dissertation.

As you have read the stories of many of my mentors throughout my life, most approach mentoring boldly and directly. Arielle's style was the exact opposite; she would quietly text me words of inspiration and encouragement. She would patiently listen to me complain about school, life, my job, my "stupid" paper. All while successfully moving on with her dissertation, getting an incredible job at her dream agency, loving life, and all things. We would meet for residences, and I would literally say, "This is stupid, I'm not going to finish, I don't want to finish," to which she would reply with positive and uplifting counter conversations. Then one day I asked, "What are you, my life coach?" We laughed and agreed that she was because that's what I needed at this stage in my life. Sometimes in life if you are being tough on yourself, what you need is a kindness coach/mentor. Someone new (like Arielle) who reminds you how fantastic you are and that you can achieve your dreams if you just stay the course and believe in yourself.

As a reminder, I have an amazing family and wonderful friends who love and support me in all the things that I do, but sometimes seeing support from a fresh set of eyes does epic things. Arielle became Dr. Woodyard and continued to inspire me and support me. Then with the support of Allen (from the last chapter), I was starting to see real progress on this monumental journey. This is when I realized the tremendous power of coaching. It was something that I had refused to implement in my own life because of [insert excuse here]. Perhaps it came from a scarcity mindset, feeling I wasn't worthy, or just plain fear of failure.

Something clicked after surviving the pandemic. I felt empowered, and I felt like with the right people on my team I could do anything. I had felt this way before in my corporate career, but working on myself, by myself (or big life goals), I was in a self-imposed moratorium that no one could/would/

should help me. When this lifted, I began to seek out people and programs that could stand in the gap for me. I was worthy of help, and marvelous professionals who love to help people were waiting to coach me to the next level.

I found a statistics coach. I enrolled in his program where I paid him to use his proven blueprint of how to finish my dissertation and to coach me across the finish line. He said a simple statement that changed my life: "You already know how to do it, or you wouldn't have got this far, all you need is a roadmap to follow." He was correct, it wasn't easy, but that's exactly what I did. During this same time, I got an ad via social media to attend a Tony Robbins live event. I mentioned earlier that his messages had always resonated with me.

We were in the middle of a pandemic, I was barely self-employed, I had just paid more for a stats coach than I paid my divorce attorney per hour, and now I was led in my spirit to attend a three-day virtual event for $700. The negative self-talk was epic for a few days, then the title of one of his previous motivational trainings popped into my heart: "Unleash the Power Within."

I did it! The energy in the event was so palpable that even my dog (love you, Bonbons) got excited and did the zoomies when Tony spoke (which if you know my pup is a rare thing, he's very laidback). Ever thought about why there are so many diets, exercise programs, self-help books, and coaching programs out there? I believe it is because we are all different and because of this diversity we are moved to action by an array of things. What moves me isn't supposed to resonate with everyone. If you tried paying for a coach or program and it didn't work, it's my firm belief that it just wasn't the right one (or the correct timing) for you—I implore you to try again!

By embracing active diversity, you can harness the full potential of your life, foster innovation and creativity, enhance engagement in your relationships, and ultimately drive better outcomes to the things that matter most in your life. Moreover, active diversity reflects a commitment to personal integrity, social responsibility, and ethical leadership; it's the right thing to do! Take a look at which table you are most often sitting at and think about what you might gain by inviting diverse people to sit with you.

> *"You have to believe it's possible and believe in yourself. Because after you've decided what you want, you have to believe it's possible, and possible for you, not just for other people. Then you need to seek out models, mentors, and coaches."* ***—Jack Canfield***

-... .-. . .- -.- .. -. --. / .- -. -.. / . -. - . .-. .. -. --.

In our journey toward personal and professional growth, it's imperative to acknowledge and confront the biases that may unconsciously influence our decisions and perceptions. This requires a willingness to examine our beliefs and attitudes with honesty and humility, recognizing that we all have blind spots that can obscure our understanding of others and ourselves. By actively seeking out diverse perspectives and experiences, engaging in meaningful conversations, and challenging our assumptions, we can begin to uncover these blind spots and expand our worldview.

At this point, I wanted to recommend nine books that everyone should read about diversity, equity, inclusion, and belonging (DEI & B). While considering this list, it struck me that my list would be chosen and speak to my biases, my circle, my environment, and my beliefs. I hope that you and I have some commonalities that drew you to read my book; however, the mentor inside me is instead going to ask you to take an action step today to identify one book, YouTube video, podcast, or training tool aiming at DEI & B education to complete by the end of this week. Our world today is filled with a plethora of free, accessible treasures to feed our minds and our souls right at our fingertips.

I will recommend one training that had a profound impact on me. Below you can see a preview of the book *What Color Are Your Jellybeans?* by Felecia Carter Harris, Ed.D.

Sneak Preview of "What Color
Are Your Jellybeans?"
by Felecia Carter Harris, Ed.D.

CHAPTER 9

The Power of No

Megan Ladd, The Changemaker

Lessons Learned from a Recovering Workaholic . . . In this final chapter, we delve into the critical counterpart to the affirmative stance explored in Chapter 1, "The Power of Yes." While embracing opportunities is crucial for growth, it's equally essential to recognize the necessity of boundaries. Without a balanced approach, saying yes to everything can lead to burnout and diminished effectiveness. Hence, mastering the art of saying no becomes paramount.

I have been blessed to have an example of this power in my spectacular daughter, Megan. Parents often say they learn important lessons from their children. In my situation, the example Megan sets for me is in stark contrast to my natural tendency to overcommit. My daughter serves as a constant reminder to me of the power of setting boundaries and saying no.

We couldn't be more different in this aspect: I, often the eager extrovert, prone to overcommitting and saying yes to every opportunity that comes my way, while she, the thoughtful introvert, has mastered the art of saying no with purpose and conviction. What started as a natural inclination for her temperament has evolved into a deliberate practice of refusing to engage in situations that may compromise her success or well-being. Whether it's at work or in her personal life, with strangers or with close family members, she navigates with grace and strength, always prioritizing her own needs and values. Her ability to assertively decline invitations or requests without guilt or hesitation is a testament to her self-awareness and unwavering integrity. Despite her quiet demeanor, she exudes strength and kindness in equal measure, her intelligence shining through in every decision she makes, and her humor bringing lightness to even the most challenging situations. In her example, I find inspiration to embrace my own boundaries and learn the value of saying no when necessary.

If you read that paragraph and had any negative thoughts about it, then you might also eat burnt toast (see Chapter 6). Understandably, some might perceive the act of setting boundaries and saying no as selfish, especially in a culture that often glorifies self-sacrifice and endless giving. However, it's essential to recognize that prioritizing one's own well-being and needs is not inherently selfish—it's an act of self-care and self-preservation. By setting boundaries and saying no, individuals are asserting their own autonomy and ensuring that they have the emotional and mental resources to thrive. In fact, it's often through practicing healthy boundaries that you can show up more fully for others in your life.

When we take care of ourselves, we are better equipped to support those around us, leading to healthier relationships and more sustainable giving. So, while it may seem counterintuitive, prioritizing personal boundaries is not selfish—it's an essential aspect of maintaining overall well-being and fostering meaningful connections with others.

Watching Megan grow into an adult and witnessing her success has taught me how powerful making yourself a priority is; it's why I gave her the title of "changemaker." I observed firsthand how it had impacted her achievements, personally and professionally. I needed to weave this example into my journey; however, change is often so very difficult.

Amid the chaos and uncertainty of the tumultuous pandemic, I found myself undergoing a profound journey of reflection. As the usual rhythms of life were disrupted and the relentless pace of daily existence slowed to a halt, I was afforded the opportunity to delve deep into the recesses of my soul. It was during these moments of introspection, during the solitude and quietude, that I began to grapple with the concept of saying no. For my health, I was forced to say no to many things during that time, despite desperately wanting to spend time with the people I loved.

For so long, I had been conditioned to prioritize the needs and expectations of others above my own, often at the expense of my own well-being. But as I navigated through the challenges and upheavals of the pandemic, I came to realize the immense power and liberation that lay in the simple act of saying no. It was a process that required introspection and a willingness to confront deeply ingrained patterns of behavior. I felt a newfound sense of empowerment and self-respect blossoming within me. Inspired by the example of Megan, I gained a deeper understanding of my boundaries, needs, and priorities, paving the way for a more authentic and fulfilling way of living.

I still struggle with time management and saying no. Yet, with each refusal uttered, I felt a newfound sense of empowerment and self-respect. Is this an area that challenges you?

Are you headed toward burnout? Here are nine warning signs that you might need to investigate: feeling overwhelmed, experiencing chronic fatigue, losing interest in activities you once enjoyed, becoming irritable or resentful, neglecting self-care, having difficulty concentrating, feeling disillusioned, experiencing physical symptoms such as headaches or stomachaches, and withdrawing from social interactions.

"Every moment that you live, first remember the true power of making decisions. It's a tool and you can use it any moment to change your entire life." —***Tony Robbins***

Scan this QR code to see my growing Small Business Toolkit:

-... .-. . .- -.- .. -. --. / .- -. -.. / . -. - . .-. .. -. --.

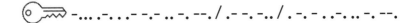

Burnout is often categorized into three main levels: mild, moderate, and severe. Here's a breakdown of each level along with their long-term effects:

1. Mild Burnout:
    - Symptoms: Mild burnout may manifest as occasional feelings of fatigue, irritability, and reduced motivation.
    - Long-Term Effects: If left unaddressed, mild burnout can progress to more severe stages. However, with early intervention and effective coping strategies, individuals can often prevent further escalation.

2. Moderate Burnout:

    - Symptoms: Moderate burnout is characterized by persistent feelings of exhaustion, cynicism, and reduced performance.
    - Long-Term Effects: Moderate burnout can lead to chronic stress, affecting physical health, emotional well-being, and interpersonal relationships. Individuals may experience increased absenteeism, reduced productivity, and difficulty managing daily responsibilities.

3. Severe Burnout:

    - Symptoms: Severe burnout involves profound physical and emotional exhaustion, feelings of detachment or apathy, and a sense of hopelessness.
    - Long-Term Effects: Severe burnout can have significant and long-lasting consequences, including depression, anxiety disorders, substance abuse, cardiovascular problems, and impaired cognitive function. It may also increase the risk of developing chronic health conditions such as hypertension, diabetes, and autoimmune disorders.

Overall, recognizing the signs of burnout and taking proactive steps to address it is crucial for mitigating its long-term effects and promoting overall well-being. Implementing self-care practices, seeking support from friends, family, or mental health professionals, and making lifestyle changes to reduce stress are essential strategies for managing burnout effectively.

If you haven't reached one of the stages of burnout above but need to balance the yes/no scale a bit more, here are nine creative ways to assert your boundaries gracefully: "I'm honored, but I'm currently at capacity," "Let me check my schedule and get back to you," "I appreciate the offer, but I need to prioritize my commitments," "I'm unable to take on any additional responsibilities at this time," "Thank you for thinking of me, but I have to decline," "I'm focusing on other priorities right now," "I'd love to, but it conflicts with my existing commitments," "I'm practicing self-care by keeping my workload manageable," and "I've learned that saying no is essential for maintaining balance in my life."

Explore the psychology behind the difficulty in saying no as part of your growth mindset. Tackling factors such as the fear of disappointing others, the desire to be perceived as helpful or accommodating, and the tendency to prioritize others' needs over our own can develop strategies to assert your boundaries confidently and effectively, ensuring your well-being and success in both personal and professional realms.

Last, here are a few technical examples of helpful tools for time management and setting boundaries:

1. Time tracking apps: Utilize apps like Toggl or RescueTime to track how you spend your time throughout the day. This can help you identify patterns, areas of improvement, and prioritize tasks effectively. I use the Timeular Physical Tracker cube to have a visual reminder that my time is valuable. It helps create tracking habits with a powerful physical reminder. Plus, as a bonus, you can view a graph of where your priorities for the day or week are.

2. Task management tools: Consider using task management tools such as Todoist, Asana, or Trello to organize your tasks and projects. These platforms allow you to create to-do lists, set deadlines, and collaborate with others, helping you stay organized and focused.

3. Calendar blocking: Implement calendar blocking techniques to allocate specific time slots for different tasks and activities. This ensures that you dedicate suf-

ficient time to important tasks and prevents overcommitting yourself.

4. Organization hacks: Utilizing tools to help you stay organized can free your brain of busy work, which gives you the power to make more beneficial decisions. Google Keep is a versatile note-taking app that allows you to capture ideas, create to-do lists, set reminders, and organize your thoughts using color-coded labels and categories. It's a convenient tool for jotting down quick notes, brainstorming, and keeping track of tasks on the go.

5. Focus your time while working: Focus@Will is a music streaming service designed to enhance productivity and focus. It provides scientifically optimized music tracks that help you concentrate, reduce distractions, and maintain mental clarity while working or studying. By listening to music tailored to your cognitive style, you can boost your productivity and stay in the zone for longer periods.

6. Email management tools: Use email management tools like Boomerang or SaneBox to prioritize and schedule emails, set reminders, and reduce email clutter. This allows you to maintain inbox zero and avoid getting overwhelmed by an overflowing inbox.

7. Automated responses: Set up automated responses or email filters to manage incoming requests and inquiries more efficiently. You can use tools like Gmail's Canned Responses feature to create pre-written responses for common inquiries or requests, saving you time and mental energy.

By leveraging these seven technical tools and strategies, you can enhance your time management skills, set boundaries more effectively, and alleviate the challenges associated with saying no. Did you notice what I did there? I did that intentionally to challenge those of you who despise change—you know who you are!

Embracing the Power & Beyond

Dr. Misty R. Sharp Ladd, CPP, PCI, PSP

The End . . . Through the pages of this book, I extend an invitation for you to glean insights, draw inspiration, and embark on your journey of growth and success guided by the principles and wisdom I've gained. May this narrative serve as a bridge between my fortunate mentorship experiences and the aspirations of those who seek to elevate their lives through mentorship, unlocking doors to possibilities they may not have imagined. Together, let us navigate the path of learning, resilience, and achievement fueled by the remarkable impact that mentorship can have on one's life.

To any of my mentees who may be reading these pages, I extend my heartfelt gratitude for allowing me the privilege of being part of your journey. Your trust, dedication, and willingness to learn have inspired me beyond measure, and I am immensely proud of the progress you have made and the growth you have achieved. As you continue to navigate your path toward success, remember that the lessons learned, the challenges overcome, and the experiences shared during our time together have equipped you with the resilience, wisdom, and determination to conquer any obstacle and seize every opportunity that comes your way. May your journey be filled with fulfillment, purpose, and endless possibilities. Here's to your continued success, both personally and professionally.

If you're ready to embark on this journey with me, stay tuned for updates on my podcast and training courses. Together, we'll dive into the world of entrepreneurship and personal development, exploring how to turn dreams into reality with flexibility and scalability at the forefront. And if you're someone who shares my passion for continuous growth and learning, I invite you to join me on this adventure. Let's connect, collaborate, and inspire each other to reach new heights. Together, we'll write the next chapter of our success stories, with mentorship guiding our way.

Simply put, I wish that you become both financially free and time free—overall happy. Embracing the techniques to harness these nine powers broken down can be your key to unlocking the life you desire and deserve. Mentors may come into your life for a reason or a season, but most will want to propel you to the next level. It will be your responsibility to get the most out of the relationship by being flexible and appreciative of the mentor's time and taking radical messy action along the way.

As you receive this transitional boost in your life, consider looking back at someone who is where you were five years ago and becoming their mentor. Remember, if you do not excel at a task, if it takes too much of your productive time, or if you don't enjoy it, consider outsourcing it.

One of my favorite television series was *Elementary*. In one of the beginning episodes, Sherlock tells Joan that no one who loves what they do needs two alarm clocks to get up in the morning. Many of us first-generation college students trying to navigate our parents' world of "hard work matters" mindset have become the most stressed-out, overworked, and unhappy people in the workforce. If you think that it's ridiculous that the next generation earns seven figures making dog videos on TikTok, I urge you to reexamine your situation. If I could trade those eighty-hour work weeks for living life showcasing how amazing Bonbons is, I would do it in an instant!

Let's be frank, you likely went into business (or your profession) because you were passionate about that one thing. The thing that sets you on fire. That makes your heart sing. The thing that makes you do a happy dance inside when you share it with other people. Opposed to a place of responsibility, duty, over-commitment, or obligation, now is the time to step into your power. The world is a vastly different place than it was before the pandemic; many people are forced to do more with less, and technological advancements have influenced every part of our lives.

With the availability of artificial intelligence (AI) tools and resources at our fingertips, I encourage you to make it easy for someone to assist you. Don't waste their time by expecting them to open long reports or read resources for you; for Pete's sake don't ask your mentor for something that you can find by simply Googling it. Your mentor wants to help you with the secret sauce, the knowledge they have spent decades creating, a deep dive into the caverns of success.

If you've tried working with a mentor before and you didn't make as much progress as you'd hoped for, perhaps you were taking too much of their time asking base-level questions. Do your homework so your mentor can help you with the hard stuff.

Focus on reciprocity; mentorship is a two-way street. I hope that you realize that success isn't confined to a specific template. Your shifting perspective can highlight your own value and potential, regardless of conventional standards. Don't think of failure as a step backward; instead, they are stepping stones toward growth. Face these challenges with resilience, perseverance, and adaptability.

At the beginning of this book, I offered you the Mentor-Mentee Action Pack cards. I would now also like to offer you a *free* additional productivity bonus. Click here to get a copy of my Small Business Action Pack Cards: https://forms.gle/zRgJj79UTmBXu1Xz9. Running a small business isn't easy, but I've got your back! These monthly actionable task cards are designed to provide you with bite-sized tasks that can make a big impact on your business growth! You can print them on cardstock, make stickers for your calendar, or upload the images to your digital reminders. Each card has a task and a time duration. Plus, I design new cards each month!

Dive into tasks that cover mindset, marketing, and momentum. Maximize productivity with just five to fifteen minutes a day. These tools help you stay on track with actionable steps for consistent growth. Say goodbye to overwhelm and hello to actionable results! I hope that you will join our community of forward-thinking entrepreneurs who are leveling up their businesses, one task at a time.

As we arrive at the culmination of this transformative journey, I extend my sincere gratitude to you, dear reader, for accompanying me through the chapters of *Breaking & Entering: Unlocking Your Path to Power Through Mentorship*. Your time and engagement are deeply appreciated. If this book has sparked moments of insight, resonated with your experiences, or ignited a newfound curiosity, I kindly ask you to share your thoughts with others. Your review holds the potential to be a guiding light for someone navigating their path of growth and mentorship. Wherever you choose to pen a few words or share your reflections, your feedback is invaluable. A review on Amazon would be spectacular, or if you prefer to send me a personal message, please connect with me via LinkedIn below.

Thank you for being an integral part of this literary expedition, and I look forward to hearing your reflections on how these pages have impacted your journey. I want to celebrate even the smallest victories with you. By recognizing and appreciating progress, we can stay motivated to continue our journey.

CONNECT WITH ME!

I would love to connect with you on LinkedIn. Scan the above code or find me at: https://www.linkedin.com/in/koiconnects

AUTHOR BIOGRAPHY

Dr. Misty R. Sharp Ladd, CPP, PCI, PSP, a distinguished Doctor of Forensic Psychology and a professional licensed private investigator, has carved a niche as an unparalleled expert in fostering the growth of solopreneurs. With a profound background as a business consultant, speaker, author, and instructor, Misty empowers entrepreneurs and students to unlock their full potential, ensuring their career trajectory is not just about growth, but consistent and impactful expansion. Leveraging a unique blend of business acumen, forensic psychology, and investigative insights, Misty crafts strategies that are both innovative and grounded in real-world application, making her a trusted facilitator for those looking to navigate the complexities of business with confidence and expertise.

Made in United States
Orlando, FL
04 May 2024

46494899R00057